"This is an important book. As you read it, you will feel your unconscious rise up and cry 'Yes! Yes!' Kat Duff has dared to give voice to the deep truth about sickness that our culture has avoided. She is a pioneer, opening up the state of illness as a new wilderness to explore. Her book has changed my life and I thank her."

Natalie Goldberg

"Sickness unto death is the resurrection of an otherwise forgotten life. Calling her with an insistent voice to a full recognition of all that was encoded in it, Kat Duff's body awakened into a consciousness that proved to be her spiritual life. With an intensity that speaks directly to the soul, this illuminating story is superbly revealed."

Marion Woodman

"Kat Duff has written a meditation born from the ache of bone against spirit. She approaches illness as a spiritual practice, a lens through which greater, darker, more beauteous and fantastic matters can be known about the Self."

Clarissa Pinkola Estés

THE ALCHEMY OF ILLNESS

Kat Duff

Bell Tower New York

Grateful acknowledgment is made to the following for permission to reprint previously published material:

Cleis Press: Excerpts from *The Absence of the Dead Is Their Way of Appearing* by Mary Winfrey Trautman. Reprinted by permission.

Copper Canyon Press: Excerpts from the poem "Nature" from *Unremembered Country* by Susan Griffin. Copyright © 1987 by Susan Griffin. Reprinted by permission of Copper Canyon Press, P.O. Box 271, Port Townsend, WA 99368.

Harcourt Brace Jovanovich, Inc.: Excerpts from "On Being Ill" in *The Moment and Other Essays* by Virginia Woolf. Copyright 1948 by Harcourt Brace Jovanovich, Inc., and renewed 1976 by Harcourt Brace Jovanovich, Inc., and Marjorie T. Parsons. Reprinted by permission of the publisher.

Station Hill Press: Excerpts from *Lupus Novice* by Laura Chester. Reprinted by permission.

Published by Bell Tower, an imprint of Harmony Books, a division of Crown Publishers, Inc.,
201 East 50th Street, New York, New York 10022.
Member of the Crown Publishing Group.
First published in 1993 by Pantheon Books.

Random House, Inc. New York, Toronto, London, Sydney, Auckland.

Bell Tower and colophon are trademarks of Crown Publishers, Inc.
Manufactured in the United States of America

DESIGN BY LAURA HOUGH

Library of Congress Cataloging-in-Publication Data
Duff, Kat, 1952–
The alchemy of illness / Kat Duff.
p. cm.
Originally published: New York, Pantheon Books, 1993.
Includes bibliographical references.
1. Sick—Psychology. 2. Medicine and psychology. 3. Chronic fatigue syndrome—Psychological aspects. 4. Social medicine.
I. Title.
R726.5.D84 1994 93-51087
155.9'16—dc20 CIP

ISBN 0-517-88097-0
10 9 8 7 6 5 4 3 2 1
First Bell Tower Edition

CONTENTS

Considering how common illness is, how tremendous the spiritual change that it brings, how astonishing, when the lights of health go down, the undiscovered countries that are then disclosed, what wastes and deserts of the soul a slight attack of influenza brings to view, what precipices and lawns sprinkled with bright flowers a little rise of temperature reveals, what ancient and obdurate oaks are uprooted in us by the act of sickness, how we go down into the pit of death and feel the waters of annihilation close above our heads and wake thinking to find ourselves in the presence of angels and the harpers when we have a tooth out and come to the surface in the dentist's armchair and confuse his "Rinse the mouth—rinse the mouth" with the greeting of the Deity stooping from the floor of Heaven to welcome us—when we think of this, as we are so frequently forced to think of it, it becomes strange indeed that illness has not taken its place with love and battle and jealousy among the prime themes of literature.

—Virginia Woolf, "On Being Ill,"
in *The Moment and Other Essays*

TO TLALTEUCTLI AND TAKÁNAKAPSÂLUK

AND ALL WHO SUFFER THAT WE MAY LIVE.

ACKNOWLEDGMENTS

While writing is a solitary pursuit, a book does not happen without the invisible labors of many people. I wish to thank Jean Thompson, whose steady faith and support carried me through the worst moments of my illness and the writing process. She was the first to encourage me to turn my thoughts into a book, never tired of discussing the ideas, and often stayed up late with a red pen in hand to edit my chapters. Sawnie Morris read early drafts with a careful critical eye and offered invaluable feedback about the writing itself, teaching me how to stay close to the truth and be kind to the reader at the same time. My brother, Chris Duff, gave me his honest responses and generous support at critical junctures. I am also grateful for the encouragement and assistance of Natalie Goldberg, who introduced me to the world of publishing and coached me much of the way. Without the help of these four individuals, this book might never have made it into print.

I also wish to thank the healing professionals who helped me find my way through the labyrinth of illness: Larry Sargent, Jacqueline Krohn, Erla Mae Larson, Frances A. Taylor, Nancy Jane

Crothers, and Martin Prechtel. I am indebted to Robert Waterman for his insights into transformational processes, to Pat and Larry Sargent, whose understanding of dreaming realities and political distortions have informed much of the method and content of this book, and to many friends and acquaintances who read early drafts and encouraged me to continue, convincing me that there was a need for this book. Finally, I feel quite fortunate to have found two strong allies and advocates in the publishing world: my agent, Ned Leavitt, and my editor, Toinette Lippe, and wish to extend my appreciation to them as well.

INTRODUCTION

In 1988 I developed what is now called chronic fatigue and immune dysfunction syndrome, or CFIDS; it is best described as a bad flu that never goes away.[1] Constant fevers, muscle aches, exhaustion, and memory lapses unraveled my life and sense of myself in a matter of months. I was often too dizzy to get up from a chair, too weak to climb a flight of stairs, too tired to talk or even listen. One day I camc out of the supermarket with a few groceries, got in my car to go home, and couldn't, for the life of me, remember where I lived, nor could I remember my phone number or figure out how to find it. Fortunately, I was so tired from standing in the checkout line that I just tilted my head back and fell asleep in my seat; when I awoke, I remembered my way home.

There is no cure as yet for CFIDS, and the only remedy is a few years of rest. While I continued to work part-time out of my home, in a feeble attempt to keep up with my bills and retain some shred of identity, I spent the better part of two years in bed. I slept twelve hours a day, and when unable to sleep, I mulled over my dreams, sifted through memories of my life, read snatches of books and magazines, and stared out the window—all the while wondering: What is the matter?

One of the oddities of being sick is that you suddenly remember all the other times you have been sick: the childhood diseases, stomach flus, allergic reactions, chest colds, food poisonings, sunstrokes . . . the list seems endless. There are minor ailments, like rashes and upset stomachs, that come and go in a matter of hours or days, serious maladies, like pneumonia or cancer, that place our lives on the line, and chronic problems—the bad back or allergies—that become lifelong companions. Illness weaves through our lives with surprising regularity. It is no less central to the human condition than sexuality is, though we hardly give it the same attention.

Memories of illness fade quickly under the glare and hubris of health, dropping into the background of life, only to rise to the forefront with the onset of yet another illness. Now that I am sick, it seems that the many and varied illnesses of my life are all simply crests on the waves of an ocean that lies beneath the surface of my world, something like a water table of the soul. When I'm well I forget it exists, but when I'm sick and sinking, I remember and return.

Illness is a familiar yet foreign landscape existing within the cosmos we inherit and inhabit as human beings, not unlike an alpine meadow or a coral reef. However, it seems to be "off the map of the knowable," as Oliver Sacks, an English neurologist, once remarked after an illness.[2] There are very few descriptions of this invisible geography, as if it were circled by a fog of forgetfulness, the thick impenetrable mists of fairy-tale lore. We hear from doctors about disease, and from a few of the formerly ill about their cures, but rarely from the sick about themselves.

I have searched through the dusty shelves of libraries and used bookstores, and scanned the small print of microfilm, for published accounts of illness, looking for the confirmation of shared experience and a few words of wisdom from those who know, but there were few to find. (Most notably, Virginia Woolf's essay "On Being Ill," E. M. Cioran's essay "On Sickness," *Tree* by Deena Metzger, *The Cancer Journals* by Audre Lorde, *Anatomy of an Illness* by Norman Cousins, *A Ray of Darkness* by Margiad Evans, *A Voice Through a Cloud* by Denton Welch, *Lupus Novice* by Laura Chester, *Wrestling with the Angel* by Max Lerner, *Body and Soul* by Albert Kreinheder, and *A Leg to Stand On* by Oliver Sacks.) Most card catalogues did not even list "illness." The experience seems to defy description, resist interpretation, and at times escape language altogether. "English," wrote Virginia Woolf, "which can express the thoughts of Hamlet and the tragedy of Lear, has no words for the shiver or the headache."[3] So illness remains a wilderness—beyond our grasp, strangely forbidding, and forever a mystery—despite its continuing presence in our lives. And like an alpine meadow or coral reef, it may play an important, even necessary, role in the ecology of the whole.

These essays evolved from notes I made during my worst years with CFIDS. I was too sick to hold complex thoughts in my mind or write whole paragraphs, but I could scribble notes and I did, about my nighttime dreams and daytime symptoms, the helpful and hurtful comments of friends, the haunting questions, secret obsessions, and unexpected revelations that come with the territory. I wrote primarily for my own survival, to steady myself within the turbulent waters of my fear and confusion, and to dispel the eerie sense of unreality and invisibility I so often felt, especially around others. (One of my earliest notes read: "I'm a buried seed unable to sprout.") But I also wrote to explore, evoke, and portray this strange territory we all visit at some point in our lives but so few recall—to remind those who are well and affirm those who are sick.

While I wrote, I also read anything and everything related to illness I could find: the diary of a nineteenth-century invalid, a scientific article on the discovery of neuropeptides (which connect our brains and immune systems), a historical account of the plague in the Middle Ages, a Buddhist treatise on cultivating the mindfulness of death, an article by a Jungian analyst on the dreams of people with cancer, an interview with a Peruvian *curandero* discussing witchcraft and curing rituals, and much more. This eclectic assortment helped me to see through the filter of scientific materialism that clouds our vision in this day and age to glimpse the deeper mysteries and hidden designs of illness. What began as a simple exploration, during which I often felt like the proverbial blind man feeling the trunk of the elephant, became a quest—a search for the meaning and purposes of illness, in my own life and in the world we share.

The essays that follow were written in the order they are presented, enabling the reader to follow the steps and stages of my quest. The first essay, "The Invisible Underworld of Illness," takes a phenomenological approach, describing the actual experience of being sick without the interference of interpretation. The remaining essays all spring from the basic ground of this beginning. The second essay, "The Secrets Our Bodies Keep Safe," investigates the unfathomable wisdom of the body in health and illness, from a stance of awe—that mixture of fear, loathing, respect, and curiosity that befalls many sick people when their bodies suddenly misbehave. In the third essay, "Toxic Health: Cultural Assumptions and Illusions," I draw upon cross-cultural perspectives and historical insights to critique popular notions of health that keep us from honoring and utilizing our illnesses.

In "Dancing with Death: Vegetative Processes at Work" I return to the dirty work of disease—the tremors, sweats, tensions, and struggles—to see what they actually accomplish during those long hours of aching, tossing, and turning that comprise the better part of our days and nights in the sickbed. The next two essays, "The Alchemy of Illness" and "The Underworld Journey," elucidate the mysterious transformations that occur under the sway of illness by comparing them to alchemical descriptions of spiritual development and the initiation rites of traditional peoples. In "Shame and the White Shadow of the Collective" I investigate the connections between the illness of an individual and the shared history and secrets of his or her people. The final essay, "Mythology and the Dark Heart of Healing," goes to the mythic core of illness and healing: the death-wielding and life-giving goddesses of the underworld who require our attention to maintain the life and world we share.

Illness, like death, is a universal experience; there is no privilege that can make us immune to its touch. However, the ways in which we construe that experience vary tremendously, depending upon the particulars of cultural context, family upbringing, and individual character. In this light, no two illnesses are the same, because no two people are alike. I have drawn extensively upon published accounts of illness and personal discussions with sick friends in an attempt to generalize beyond the parameters of my own experience; however, I am sure that the particulars of my situation, as a white woman of sufficient means and mystical temperament nearing forty in twentieth-century America, inform my vision of health and illness in ways I cannot begin to understand. I have no desire to impose interpretations on people and processes that are so complex and various; my only hope is to restore mystery and dignity to the experience of being sick.

Margiad Evans, one of my favorite chroniclers of illness, wrote in her autobiography: "Our health is as a voyage: and every illness is an adventure story."[4] So we begin the adventure.

THE ALCHEMY OF ILLNESS

1

THE INVISIBLE UNDERWORLD OF ILLNESS

Silenced, she sank easily through deeps under deeps of darkness until she lay like a stone at the farthest bottom of life, knowing herself to be blind, deaf, speechless, no longer aware of the members of her own body, entirely withdrawn from all human concerns, yet alive with a peculiar lucidity and coherence; all notions of the mind, the reasonable inquiries of doubt, all ties of blood and the desires of the heart, dissolved and fell away from her, and there remained of her only a minute fiercely burning particle of being that knew itself alone, that relied upon nothing beyond itself for its strength.

—Katherine Anne Porter[1]

I lie sprawled across my bed, as if thrown aimlessly aside. The trappings of illness surround me: a litter of twisted tissues and covers, half-empty glasses of water (one with a fly floating in it), and plastic pill bottles. I have been watching clouds of dust swim through the slanting rectangle of light from my window for quite some time. The silence is so deep it reminds me of interstellar space, of vast swirling seas of cosmic debris, the leftover stuff of creation.

I have heard myself say—at that moment of realizing I am

getting sick, with the slim chill of a fever or the sudden revulsion of nausea—"Oh, yes, I remember this place." Illness is a world of its own, another plane of reality, that is quite apart from the one we normally inhabit in the ordinary dailiness of health. It has its own geography "beneath deeps of darkness," its own gravity "at the farthest bottom of life," its own laws and commandments that strip us of "all notions of the mind . . . and the desires of the heart." And it offers an extraordinary—if at times frightening—vantage point from which to view the terrain of one's life.

I have been quite surprised to discover since I've been sick with CFIDS that the world of illness is not deathly boring, as I would have imagined from the lofty heights of health, but surprisingly interesting once you're up close and inside it, in the same way that a desolate desert landscape comes alive with night-flowering cacti and scuttling scorpions under careful scrutiny. More than interesting, illness seems crucial, heavy with meaning and import, in ways I can hardly explain, but will attempt to do so in the following chapters. Let me begin by describing the curious terrain of the sick with the immediacy and intimacy of one who is living inside its borders.

THE WASTES AND DESERTS OF THE SOUL

There are few indelible facts about illness, but one thing is certain: No one chooses to get sick. In fact, we avoid it like the plague with our rituals and regimens of healthy living. Illness chooses us, instead, for its own inscrutable reasons, just as surely as the clouds catch up with the sun to cast a net of darkness upon the land. We are caught unsuspecting by the onset of symptoms, and often feel attacked or persecuted, even slain, by this stealthy burglar, this hungry hunter, who has made us its prey. Occasionally we sense the hunter's approach, feel the sudden pall of the encroaching shadow, and complain of feeling a little under the weather, but by then it's usually too late; we've already been taken, abducted like Persephone into the underworld of sickness. As John Donne, who was sick for many years, observed, "Health is a long and regular work (we polish every stone that goes into that building); but sickness summons us, seizes us, possesses us and destroys us in an instant."[2]

I cannot remember much of the days and months I was sliding down into the illness I now have, but I do remember very clearly the exact time and place I landed. It was a warm, gray day in the spring of 1988 in Austin, Texas. I had just finished a counseling session with a client; when he shut the door behind him, I sat back in my chair with a great sigh and noticed, for the first time, the intricate, mazelike patterns on the Persian rug at my feet. As I stared at those dizzying patterns, I felt myself sinking, like an anchor at sea, with exhaustion and decided to lie down for a few minutes.

I woke up an hour later with my face pressing into the scratchy surface of the rug. My clothes were wet with sweat, my heart raced at an irregular tempo, and I could not figure out where I was or the time of day. The doorbell rang, and I thought about answering, but could not muster the will or strength to get up. Eventually I got my bearings, sat up, and called a friend, but I knew I had fallen, like an old tree in the depths of a dark and silent forest, and even though I managed to get up off the floor that afternoon, I never really got up again.

We do not dip our feet into the waters of illness; we are fully immersed in them, as if pulled under by a relentless undertow. As we become sick, sickness becomes us and redefines us, so we say we are not ourselves anymore. In a few short hours I was transformed from a hardworking counselor and avid swimmer into a "patient"—one hundred pounds of warm, white, shuddering flesh. The next morning I sat on a metal examining table in the doctor's office, shivering under the tent of my paper gown, dreading the verdict.

In the onslaught of illness we drop the distinguishing apparel of our daily lives to assume the uniform dress of the sick: glazed eyes, matted hair, stale smells, and wan expression.

Illness is an upside-down world, a mirror image reversing the assumptions of our normal daily lives. I think of it as the underside of life itself, the night to our days, the roots of our trees. The first thing that happens when I get sick, even before physical symptoms appear, is that I lose my usual interests. A kind of existential ennui rises in my bones like floodwaters, and nothing seems worth doing: making breakfast, getting to work on time, or making love. That is when I know I am succumbing to the influence of illness, whether it is a minor cold or a life-threatening case of dysentery. I slip, like fluid through a porous membrane, into the nightshade of my solar self, where I am tired of my friends, I hate my work, the weather stinks, and I am a failure.

Sometimes I ask myself, "Why didn't I see this before?" Then some sure voice from the depths of my illness replies, "You could not see before."

That sure voice fills me with a shuddering awe I have come to associate with moonless nights, pounding surf, and other such imposing presences. She holds no allegiance to my preferred self-concepts and proud accomplishments; in fact, she seems to enjoy replaying recent events in a humiliating light during those long, insufferable afternoons in bed. "The past rises like a tide," wrote May Sarton while recovering from a stroke, "over and over, to swamp me with memories I cannot handle. . . ."[3] That sure voice seems to remember everything we have forgotten, overlooked, or slipped under the rug: our original purposes, deflected desires, and occasional failures.

During one such afternoon, when the winter light was so bright I had to close the curtains, I thought back to a workshop I had given the year before on the interplay of shame, sexuality, and spirituality. While the workshop went well, ostensibly, the scenes I remembered that afternoon made me cringe with embarrassment.

I saw myself sitting cross-legged on the floor facing a half-circle of workshop participants, leaning forward intently to listen, searching my mind for the "right" thing to say in response. The image reminded me of a young woman I know who was brain-injured at birth; she often "reads" with her family by sitting down with a book in her lap and turning the pages slowly, one by one, even though she cannot read and, more often than not, her book is upside-down. She and I both assume earnest, studious appearances when we have no idea what we are doing. That sure voice whispered in my ear, "Who do you think you are?"

As I lay in my bed, aching with embarrassment and fever, I understood the extent of my own ignorance and folly, my ever-so-human inadequacies. Other stark afternoons and dismal early mornings brought more memories filled with regret, during which I had to face the fact that I did not have the courage to visit an old friend when she was hospitalized with a nervous breakdown, or the self-respect to pursue my creative inclinations, despite repeated opportunities. These are what Virginia Woolf called the "wastes and deserts of the soul" that appear "when the lights of health go down."[4] I often emerge from that desolate vision feeling very small, bound by the circle of my own limitations, and beset by the handmaidens of illness: doom, depression, and despair.

I recently watched a friend slip into those clutches of doom in a matter of seconds during an allergic reaction to something she ate at Thanksgiving; we were chatting over coffee when she jumped to her feet, tore off her sweater, shoes, and socks, and began scratching her arms and legs furiously, shouting, "I'm burning up all over, I'm dying!" While we burst out laughing at the time, responses like hers are not unwarranted; after all, people die from allergic reactions all the time. Under the influence of illness we are made privy to the forbidden knowledge of the immediacy of death that separates the sick and dying from the young and healthy. Illness confers, as philosopher E. M. Cioran once noted, "the experience of the terrible."[5]

Since I have been sick, I have encountered some truly terrifying possibilities: that I am dying, for one; that the man who molested me when I was a baby wishes me dead, and that the nuclear research lab nearby is emitting radiation that is killing all of us. Friends call it paranoia, and so do I sometimes, while at other times I wake in a cold sweat, sure that it is absolutely true and hidden by a conspiracy of silence, the web of denial that is spun by those who have never known tragedy. I have spent hours in the middle of the night making out my will, deliberating over whether to be cremated or buried, crying big tears over the loss of my friends and family, only to resolve suddenly that I would not give my molester the satisfaction of my death!

When the thermometer reads over 100 degrees, which, as my mother taught me when I was little, means I am *really* sick, I am tempted to discount these frightening images and depressing thoughts as some sort of biochemical disturbance, which of course they are. Living with a chronic illness, in which some days are better than others, constantly reminds me that my mood and outlook follow the swings of my energy level with uncanny precision. So I try to distract myself with light reading (mail-order catalogues work best) and household tasks, but they do not work for long with the short attention spans of illness. That sure voice returns to insist something is seriously amiss—not so much in my illness as in the so-called health that preceded it.

Sick people often allude to the limitations of what we know as health, the one-sidedness of its ready optimism and confidence, the withering effects of its constant activity and interaction. English author Margiad Evans, who developed epilepsy as an adult, wrote that "too much health is like too much light; it blinds," later explaining that "the epileptic seems to be in constant communion . . . with a general and dark source of being."[6] Illness pulls our awareness into the deepest recesses of self; from that perspective, our previous lives of busy well-being often seem misguided.

Since I have been sick and staying home most of the time,

I have often wondered why I used to dash around in my little 1981 Toyota, from meetings to movies, grocery stores to post offices, with such fervent zeal. One day, when I was resting on the couch after a trip to the post office, I saw in my mind's eye the path my car has taken in all its travels as the zigzag of a time-lapse photograph; it resembled the skitter of a moth mesmerized by a light bulb, the scattered flight of a chicken with its head cut off. Suddenly I understood what my elderly Hispanic neighbor, a fifth-generation sheepherder, means when he shakes his fist at speeding cars and shouts, "What's the hurry? What's so important?"

I find it very difficult to reconcile the contrary visions of health and illness, or even hold them both in my mind at the same time. They slip away from each other, like oil and water. After a few months in bed I could not remember what it felt like to swim a mile, which I used to do almost every day. I had forgotten the pleasure of cool water on my skin, the comfort of a smooth stroke; I could only imagine it to be cold and exhausting from the vantage point of my warm water bed and interminable fatigue. It happens the other way around too. A friend of mine who is recovering from CFIDS confided the other day, "I'm afraid I'll forget what it was like; I already do on my good days." It is like trying to remember the deep freeze of winter when you are sweltering on the beach in August. Our brains are not well equipped for such exercises, but something compels us to make the effort, to hold contrary pictures in a single vision.

I have heard it said that illness is an attempt to escape the truth. I suspect it is actually an attempt to embody the whole truth, to remember all of ourselves. For illness is not just something that happens to us, like a sudden sneeze or passing storm; it is part of who we are all the time. We carry within ourselves all the diseases we have had, and many we will have, as genetic inclinations, damaged organs, hidden bacteria, and sleeping cancer cells. We just rise above these realities in the heyday of health—only to sink back down into their murky depths when disease takes over.

STRANGE VISITATIONS AND UNEXPECTED TRANSFORMATIONS

Under the sway of illness, people, like food, lose their appeal. Simple tasks, such as getting dressed, making meals, or returning phone calls, become difficult and onerous duties we avoid whenever possible. Our tolerances shrink to a narrow span; the juice is too sweet, the refrigerator too loud, the sheets too cold. I used to enjoy listening to the radio while working at my desk, but once I got sick, I could not stand the noise; I felt crowded and exhausted by it. That is why sick people spin cocoons around themselves; I often imagine myself wrapped like a mummy in a thick, fluffy blanket that filters out the invasive noises and smells of daily life.

We shut the door, pull the shades, and unplug the phone when illness strikes, slipping away from the outer world and its material seductions like a boat drifting out to sea. The detailed terrain of our usual lives fades into a thin line between the vast indifferent fields of sea and sky in the underworld of illness. We have nothing to say or do and want only to be left alone.

The interiority of illness makes its own compelling sounds—a steady humming, thick silence, or terrible ringing—that drown out the common engaging noises of life, the kitchen conversations and crying children. There have been many times when I have found it nearly impossible to focus my attention on anything outside of myself, because I was so preoccupied with my own discomfort: a swirling dizziness, haunting memory, or approaching panic. The life/death struggle that is illness is utterly consuming; we are possessed by it, and everything else pales by comparison. Simone de Beauvoir reported that when her mother was sick with cancer she interrupted a friend who had started to tell a lively piece of gossip to say, "You ought not to tell sick people stories of that kind; it doesn't interest them."[7] It is difficult to reach across the gulf that surrounds a sick person with words or touch. Either they fall into the yawning gap unnoticed or they pierce the veil and come too close, as if violating some sacred boundary.

There is, perhaps rightly so, an invisible rope that separates the sick from the well, so that each is repelled by the other, like magnets reversed. The well venture forth to accomplish great deeds in the world, while the sick turn back onto themselves and commune with the dead; neither can face the other very comfortably, without intrusions of envy, resentment, fear, or horror. Frankly, from the viewpoint of illness, healthy people seem ridiculous, even a touch dangerous, in their blinded busyness, marching like soldiers to the drumbeat of duty and desire.

Their world, to which we once belonged and will again most likely, seems unreal, like some kind of board game that could fold up at any minute. Carl Jung reported that when he was recovering from a heart attack, the view from his window seemed "like a painted curtain with black holes in it, or a tattered sheet of newspaper full of photographs that meant nothing." He despaired of getting well and having to "convince myself all over again that this was important!"[8] We drop out of the game when we get sick, leave the field, and desert the cause. I often feel like a ghost, the slight shade of a person, floating through that world, but not of it. The rules and parameters of my world are different altogether.

Space and time lose their customary definitions and distinctions. We drift in a daze and wake with a start to wonder: Where am I? On the train to San Francisco or at Grandmother's house? Maybe both, for opposites coexist in the underworld of illness. We are hot and cold at once, unable to decide whether to throw off the blankets or pile more on, while something tells us our lives are at stake. Sometimes I feel heavy as a sinking ship, and other times light as a spirit rising from the wreckage. Our worlds shrink down to the four walls of the sickroom; then entire universes unfurl themselves in the dust swirling above the bed.

Time stretches and collapses, warping like a record left in

the sun. After living with epilepsy for several years, Margiad Evans wrote, "Time has come to mean nothing fixed to me: in certain moods it seems I slip in and out of its meshes as a sardine through a herring net."[9] Ten seconds seems like an hour of torture in acute pain, while a whole lifetime can squeeze into a few moments as we wake from sleep or fall in a faint. Past and future inhabit the present, like threads so tangled the ends cannot be found. There have been times, in that liminal realm between sleep and waking, when my life appeared before me as the shifting patterns of a weaving pulled by the corners, or the flickering reflections in an oil slick. What has been and what could be stand side by side without distinction; strange things seem connected.

Many years ago I had a curious experience when I was sick with a fever in a tiny efficiency apartment in Santa Fe. I was drifting in and out of sleep, to the din of fiestas outside, when a host of images swept before me like a flock of birds: a long list of the addresses of my life, the kitchen windows and back stoops I had loved, the stars of the Big Dipper turning overhead, all the boxes, so many cardboard boxes, carried in and out of houses. Suddenly I knew that I did not have to keep moving every two years, as I had my entire adult life. I saw the skin of my restlessness rise from my body, like the thin trickle of smoke from a pipe. Sure enough, the next move was my last to date.

Nan Shin, an American Zen nun, described a similar experience, in which several odd and unrelated events of her past converged in her mind to make a new pattern, when she was sick with cancer. She described it in her diary: "I sat zazen pretty regularly, and one evening there was an obscure movement of molecules . . . that had to do with my relationship with my mother, our uneasy inability to unhook from each other, and with my own refusal to have children, and in which floated the concluding sentence of a tiny French book by an ex-Lacanian woman analyst about mother-daughter relationships; the sentence is something like, If only I could live without your having to die." It was "yet another jolt," she wrote, adding, "I relate all this because it shows what kind of [healing] process I followed, which was haphazard but on all fronts at once. I would recommend it."[10]

The underworld of illness is full of such impossible events, strange visitations, and unexpected transformations. When I was sick with fever and exhaustion after finals my first year of graduate school, a favorite uncle, who was in a coma at the time, appeared to me in what I can only call his angelic form; he smelled of bourbon and cigarettes, as always, but radiated an extraordinary, effervescent light and communicated a love for me that totally dispelled the guilt I felt over the circumstances surrounding his heart attack. When I was sick with dysentery in India, barely able to lift my head, a Hindu holy man in orange appeared in the corner of my hotel room and sent healing waves of energy through my ragged body.

Defying the rules of ordinary reality, illness shares in the hidden logic of dreams, fairy tales, and the spirit realms mystics and shamans describe. There is often the feeling of exile, wandering, searching, facing dangers, finding treasures. Familiar faces take on the appearance of archetypal allies and enemies, "some putting on a strange beauty, others deformed to the squatness of toads," as Virginia Woolf noted.[11] Dreams assume a momentous authority, while small ordinary things, like aspirin, sunshine, or a glass of water, become charged with potency, the magical ability to cure or poison.

Sick people often identify causes for their ailments that their family and friends find unbelievable, such as the wind, nuclear radiation, or a bad marriage. My parents have learned to nod along when I offer my latest theory about the underlying cause of my immune deficiency, whether it is parasites from India, the mercury fillings in my teeth, or family karma, but the fact is that they are all true in the strange coordinates of this illness. Cures are equally unbelievable. Who would imagine that someone could recover from a terminal case of cancer by receiving massive doses of radiation, or drugs first developed for chemical warfare, much less by watching funny movies? I have begun to suspect that in the otherworld reality of illness, anything and everything can kill and heal, whether it is digitalis in heart medicine, a lover's touch, or God's grace. There is no apparent rhyme or reason to the geography of illness, only the ultimate authority and agency of physical pain.

PRIVATE TORTURES AND THE WATERS OF FORGETFULNESS

Sometimes I like to hide in the magical invisibility of illness and listen to private conversations or watch my lover dress in front of the mirror. But inevitably a loud question or a cold hand on my forehead breaks the spell and exposes me, like a fugitive caught in the frame of a roving searchlight. My secrets leak out of me, in the untouched food, the soaked sheets, the disjointed words—the many small indignities of illness—inviting the critical scrutiny of those who wonder what the matter is. The matter is me, my body, naked yet unseen, covered and revealing. In illness there is the fact that we cannot hide in our bodies or from our bodies, and also the burning desire to do so.

There comes that point when the symptoms—the headache, congestion, or nausea—is so uncomfortable, so painful, that we cannot think of anything else. Our usually free and wide-ranging consciousness is focused, fixed, indeed nailed to that point in our bodies calling attention. The whole world collapses into that point and ceases to exist; for pain is the sword that clears everything away, the sudden swish of annihilation. As Emily Dickinson put it, "Pain has an element of blank."[12] Questions go unanswered, sentences unfinished. The water we put on for tea boils away, forgotten. In the urgency of pain language itself is shattered; we are reduced to the cries and murmurs of a preverbal state. No wonder pain so often attends and enables our dying.

I am not sure what, if anything, happens in that consuming black hole of sudden pain; a friend of mine says that old spooks rush out and new ones come in while our censors are down. I have noticed that my world looks a little different, as if slightly rearranged by some mysterious sleight of hand, when I finally stand up after vomiting or emerge from the delirium of a high fever: Colors seem brighter, the angle of the ceiling looks skewed, everything is funny or unbearably sad. I have often felt as though a few feet of my lifeline had been cut off by the silent scissors of fate, taking me one giant step closer to my death.

I suppose it is human, particularly human, to resist pain and feel unjustly accused. I twist and turn, flopping about like a fish on the line, cursing out loud, until finally, exhausted, I surrender to stillness. I imagine that instruments of torture—knives, rakes, ropes, and hammers—are assaulting my body, and think of Prometheus chained to a rock while vultures picked at his liver, and of Jesus nailed to the cross in the hot sun. Every illness, minor or major, is a crucible that tries our metal and tests our limits. I am often shocked to realize how quickly a small cold or flu, even a headache can unhinge me, and make me pray for mercy or beg for drugs from gods and doctors I ordinarily have no time for.

Once in a while pain gives way, like a trapdoor, into a hidden pool of grace. I lie perfectly still when it happens, because I am afraid to believe it is true, and suspicious or superstitious enough to think that a small tilt of my head or twist of my foot could dispel this miraculous state of grace. In that sudden stillness and unexpected calm, everything around me—the spider slipping into a crack in the wall, the twig scratching my window—seems to partake of an enduring perfection. Unfortunately, these moments of reprieve and revelation slip away as quickly as they come, to leave me groping the wall of pain once again. That is when bitterness brews; I feel tricked and betrayed by my own body and by the gods who seem to have turned their backs on me without a moment's regret. Most people who live with a chronic illness will tell you that relapses are made much worse by the fact that they follow temporary remissions, when we think, with the eternal optimism of well-being, that we have escaped the clutch of pain for good.

Nothing is more real than pain when we are in its clutches. English author Denton Welch wrote that this thought appeared "like a text in cross-stitch" when he lay in agony in the hospital after being hit by a car. "I wanted to warn the nurses," he continued, "to tell them that nothing was real but torture. Nobody seemed to realize that this was the only thing on earth."[13] There is a curious paradox that surrounds pain: Nothing is more certain to those afflicted, while nothing is more open to question and doubt by others.[14]

Most varieties of pain are invisible and incommunicable; they reside within the depths of our bodies as private tortures, leaving few traces on the skin for others to see. Even when evidence exists, as in swollen joints or surgical stitches, people often prefer not to comment or ask questions, perhaps in order to protect the privacy of pain, perhaps to deny its existence altogether. Almost everyone has had the experience of telling a friend, relative, or doctor about some ailment, only to be met with that ingratiating "yes, dear" nod usually reserved for babbling two-year-olds, or cut short by a demand to see the records, or even accused of making it up. People often say, "You're just tired" or "depressed," that "It will be over in no time" or "All you need is a good night's sleep." And while these sayings may prove true at times, we feel doubly betrayed, by our bodies and by others.

Pain, whether it is physical or emotional, drives a wedge between private and public realities that the psyche has difficulty straddling. Many people describe pain as "splitting," with attending sensations of burning or crawling on the skin itself, the organ that mediates between public and private realms. I often feel I am lying when I answer, "Fine," with a smile in response to the popular "How are you?" greeting, even though I am still running a fever and my lymph nodes are swollen and pounding, but I also felt like a fraud when I truthfully answered on a particularly bad day, "I'm miserable, my whole body hurts, my brain won't work, and I wish I were dead," because such sentiments do not belong in public. Moreover, they are not very believable when they come from someone who looks fine. I once stood in line for forty-five minutes to renew my driver's license, even though my legs were trembling and my vision blurring with dizziness, rather than take one of the chairs reserved for the elderly, because I was afraid no one would believe that someone so young and healthy-looking as I really needed a chair.

Public and private realities are irreconcilable in the midst of profound anguish; when pain subsides, the psyche often chooses one version of truth over the other. I have noticed that whenever I have a good day or week, I jump to the conclusion that I am finally getting over this awful disease, and I race around doing all those things I could not do before: clean windows, visit friends, see a movie, or go hiking. It seems that some part of me is always ready to forget the facts of my illness, to spread a film of amnesia over this open wound and adopt a more convenient, socially acceptable reality: that I am now well. Friends and acquaintances are equally eager to welcome me back to the world of the living, telling me I look great, even when my skin is still hanging off my bones and a gust of wind could blow me over.

Because the experience of illness is so difficult to accept, communicate, and integrate, it sinks into the mute flesh of our bodies as we recover. In fact, the word "recover" literally means "to cover up again." We lose that piece of our lives, that corner of truth, in order to reclaim the world we share with others. The experience may be forgotten altogether, or obscured by the workings of memory into the shadows of insignificance, with euphemistic understatements like "It was just a bad dream" or "I had a little trouble with my heart." It appears that the terrain of the sick, like the underworld in Greek mythology, is surrounded by the waters of forgetfulness.

Our tendency to whitewash the details of disease may be a

natural—even necessary—phenomenon, the psychological equivalent to the formation of scar tissue, but it cannot restore the smooth skin of innocence. Our worlds are changed by the experience of illness, and so are we, indelibly marked by the ordeal, just as the heroes of Greek mythology cannot escape the underworld without paying a price or making a sacrifice. The changes we endure in the midst of illness will be explored in greater detail in future chapters; let it suffice to say that no one returns from an operation, accident, or major illness exactly the same; there is a bitterness or compassion, strength or fragility, faith or despondency, that was never there before.

However, unlike passing ailments, long-lasting illnesses do not allow us the luxury of forgetting the details of disease for long, for they return with a vengeance in a matter of hours, weeks, or months. Since I have been sick with chronic fatigue, I have paid dearly for my habit of forgetting with countless relapses. When I ignore the early signals of fatigue in the ecstasy of a good day or the determination to get something done, I tend to overextend myself, only to land back in bed, crying with exhaustion and a rising fever—and it can take me weeks to regain the strength I had so carefully cultivated up to that point.

After many such cycles of excess and relapse, I have trained myself to a path of moderation, curtailing my activities to that small circle—a radius of twenty miles from my home—that I know I can comfortably inhabit. I sit rather than stand, stay put rather than move, go deeper rather than farther, whenever I can, to conserve my energies and quicken my recovery, but also because I have been doing it for so long now that it has become my habit, even my preference. CFIDS has changed me, for better or for worse. To some, it may look as though I am clinging to my illness, but to me it is the better part of valor to agree to one's fate and allow oneself to be transformed—twisted and transfigured—by that which we will never fully understand.

2

THE SECRETS OUR BODIES KEEP SAFE

What is really feared is an open door into a consciousness which leads us back to the old, ancient, infant and mother knowledge of the body, in whose depths lies another form of culture not opposed to nature but instead expressing the full power of nature and our natures.

—Susan Griffin[1]

In October 1989, when the earthquake struck California, I was sick in bed, where I had been for the past six months, running a fever and losing my memory, much to my horror. My friend Alicia was outside of Santa Cruz, only two miles from the epicenter of the quake, driving home from work, when all the cars on the highway, including hers, began hopping "like jelly beans." A month later I got a letter from Alicia, in which she wrote, in an especially heavy scrawl, "I'll never fully trust the ground again." I remember her words exactly, because I thought to myself at the time, I'll never fully trust my body again.

I was wrong. Now, only two years later, I find that I trust my body more than I ever did before I got sick. The trust I have now is not a cavalier expectation of health—I suspect that *is* gone for good—but a deep respect for the ancient weight and wisdom of my body—which I had failed to notice when I was feeling fine.

OF IGNORANCE AND AWE

"A man in good health," observed E. M. Cioran, "collapses into well-being, an insignificant state of perfection, of impermeability to death as well as of inattention to oneself and the world."[2] When our bodies obey without a complaint we take them for granted; what passes for trust is really blithe ignorance and the unconscious presumption that our bodies are somehow "with" us, even under our command. Illness shatters that illusion. When my body suddenly revolts like a bucking horse—breaking out in hives, crumpling in a faint, or refusing the dinner I just ate—I am often shocked to realize it has a will of its own perfectly capable of supplanting my own. Sometimes I feel betrayed by this being I thought was my ally, and protest vehemently, like an aging autocrat cornered in his office in the midst of a political coup: "Why me? Why now? What's wrong? This isn't fair!" I have even wondered, amid the sudden reversals of disease, whether some alien being has taken possession of my body—a fantasy which the metaphors of modern medicine, with its "viral invasions" and "arsenal" of drugs, encourage.

However, much as illness resembles a hostile takeover, possession cannot occur unless the body allows it, just as a good marriage cannot be broken by the "other" man or woman unless it is already cracking. So the question remains: Why the sudden infidelity? As I pondered this question in the fall of 1989, during the long hours of rest my doctor ordered, I realized that I did not really know this small-boned and blue-eyed being I live with day in and day out; she was a stranger to me, a stranger I had married at birth till death do us part for some forgotten reason. The experience reminded me of those rare moments in a marriage when you wake up, startled, to realize that the person lying next to you in bed is not the person you thought you knew. I had to admit that I knew very little of what goes on inside my body, of what it wants or needs, why it does what it does, or even where its allegiances lie.

One day, when I glanced in the bedroom mirror in passing, I did not recognize myself at first; I stopped short, stepped back, and examined the well-worn and graying face in the mirror with a newfound curiosity, as if she were someone else, a new acquaintance. At times like these, when the veil of our self-definitions dissolve—even for a second—a sense of mystery arises where there was none before, for what was once faded with familiarity becomes fresh with the strangeness of unfamiliarity. It is as if some film were lifted from our eyes, enabling us to see more closely and accurately. That is when true relationship becomes possible.

When I was examining my face that day—or perhaps it was another day—I noticed, for the first time ever, that one of my eyes is open and trusting, and the other squinting and suspicious, as if the trunk of my life's experience had been split in two. The realization of this fundamental schism in my being, reflected in the telltale clues of my body, stunned me, and I pondered it for days. One could say that I truly recognized myself in that moment, and so began a more conscious relationship with my body and the hidden, forgotten parts of myself.

I have never spent so much time—except perhaps when I was a teenager—investigating my body as I have since I have been sick. With the inquisitiveness of an explorer, the solicitousness of a mother, and the tenderness of a lover, I place the back of my hand on my forehead to check my temperature, finger the swollen lymph nodes in my neck and groin, rub my thighs and massage my abdomen, pull up the skin on my forearm just because it is so loose, stick out my tongue in the mirror to see if it's coated, sense the weariness of my skeleton when I relax, and even imagine the parasites that colonized my intestines squirming like snakes in a rabbit hole. I keep a running dialogue with my body the way children do with their imaginary friends, cursing ("Damn it! You left the stove on again"), pleading ("Please, give me the strength to get up this hill"), and praising ("Congratulations! You filled the woodbox all by yourself!"). I also ask questions—"Can I eat ice cream?" "Can I go for a swim?"—and watch carefully for signs of an answer, noticing my body's responses to a spoonful of ice cream, the smell of car exhaust, or the sound of classical music.

I remember staring at an infected paper cut on the palm of my hand one cold November afternoon, frightened that my immune system was so weak it could no longer heal a paper cut without difficulty, but also incredulous, for the first time in my life, that it ever could; illness often spawns this awe of the body's abilities, simply because they appear to be faltering. Since I have been sick, I have sometimes thought of my body as an old, beat-up Chevy pickup, sputtering down the road on a few cylinders. But this day was different. When I looked closely at that infected paper cut, I saw that it crossed over a thin white line, the scar that remained from the day when I was eight years old and the doctor cut open my hand to retrieve a buried sliver. I remembered the experience quite clearly, because it was the first time in my life I actually saw the raw flesh of my insides; it was a gut-wrenching revelation of my physicality, my animal vulnerability, and I fainted.

While staring at my hand and thinking of that incident on that cold, clear November afternoon, I suddenly understood that my body was not broken, like an old Chevy, but remembering, like a mother.

FOSSIL MEMORIES

Our bodies remember it all: our births, the delights and terrors of a lifetime, the journeys of our ancestors, the very evolution of life on earth. I discovered several years ago that there is a point on the inside of my knee that holds the memory and fear of a time when I was a baby and some big person lay on top of me, which I do not consciously remember. But when someone presses that point, I am suddenly there, squirming and struggling for air. Apparently I'm not the only one with trigger points for memories dotting my body like towns on a map, for gynecologist Christiane Northrup has noted that women often have memories of forgotten incest experiences during pelvic exams, explaining that procedures like these can stir up "cellular memory, the information locked in our bodies."[3]

Our immune systems carry the memory of each and every virus we have ever encountered; in fact every experience, from the sight of a field of daisies to the sudden shock of cold water, leaves a chemical footprint in the body, shimmering across the folds of the cortex like a wave across water, altering our attitudes, expectations, memories, and moods ever so slightly in a continual process of biological learning. Deepak Chopra, an Ayurvedic physician and M.D., offered a helpful analogy to describe this process by which experiences are literally embodied: "The minutes of life (the sorrows, joys, fleeting seconds of trauma, and long hours of nothing special at all) silently accumulate and, like grains of sand deposited by a river, the minutes can eventually pile up into a hidden formation that crops above the surface" as individual variations of health and illness: the straight back, wheezing cough, or fluctuating blood sugar.[4]

Chopra also made the intriguing observation that "Memory is more permanent than matter," since formations like scars remain after all the cells that compose them are replaced, and concluded, "Your body is just the place your memory calls home." This would explain how our bodies retain the memories of experience that precede our births. Recently a friend told me that when she visited the hills of Kentucky, where ancestors on both sides of her family had lived for generations, she felt an uncanny sense of familiarity, a sinking relaxation in her body, as if it remembered that landscape once called home. Another friend recalled that she developed a sudden terror of heights at age forty-five, only to learn that her grandfather had watched a woman fall to her death from a tall building when he was that age. The body, it would seem, is a living history book.

The history encoded in our bodies is not just personal; it is also collective. Our brains contain the smaller brains of our reptilian and mammalian ancestors, what the Cherokee call our "snake and turtle minds," and we repeat their wiggling, crawling, and swinging movements in infancy, dance, and sexual play. I once looked across a room of people dancing and saw, instead, monkeys swinging from branches, otters ducking in the waves, turtles waddling across the road, and snakes slithering into rabbit holes. We also repeat these instinctual, autonomic movements in illness, when we are shivering uncontrollably, heaving over the toilet, rocking with pain, or crawling out of bed with a headache. Perhaps that is why we often speak of being reduced by illness into crybabies, slovenly beasts, or inert vegetables. Every one of us has been a tree, a fish, a deer, and much more, as the Buddhists insist, and we continue to be these things.

Sick people often speak of "crawling back through the ages" of memory, like archeologists searching for hidden origins; as Elie Wiesel noted, "When one is ill or mad, one wants to look back as far as possible: to the brink. And beyond. Until one is back as far as possible, until one transcends that beginning."[5] When I was sickest, I lost interest in many of my usual studies, but developed a passion for reading creation myths, reveling in images of vast swirling seas of darkness, spiders spinning cosmic threads, golden eggs bursting open, a big bang at the start of time. I suspect it is no coincidence that Charles Darwin developed his theory of evolution while nearly crippled with headaches, and the renowned physicist Stephen Hawking, who has devoted his life to figuring out how the universe began, has an advanced case of Lou Gehrig's disease. Nor is it a coincidence that the healing rituals of many traditional peoples include the retelling of creation stories.

Scientists now say that our bodies, like everything else on earth, contain atoms from the beginning of time and the origins of our universe. The elements that form our physical makeup are the same ones that constitute the earth as a living body—seawater and volcanic ash, circulating air and the spark of life that is fire—and they rank among the most powerful agents for healing, as the popularity of mineral hot springs around the world testifies. "The body is a part of the earth," explained Dr. Lewis E. Mehl, a Cherokee physician and healer. It is "the earthly home for the soul. It knows more about life on earth than the mind. When in doubt, we ask the body."[6]

My body has taught me many things, all of them filled with soul: how to dance and make love, mourn and make music; now it is teaching me how to heal. I am learning to heed the shifting currents of my body—the subtle changes in temperature, muscle tension, thought, and mood—the way a sailor rides the wind by reading the ripples on the water. Sometimes I am surprised by the feedback my body gives me; after being a vegetarian for twelve years I was astonished—and mortified—to discover that my body thrives on an occasional serving of organic red meat, at least for now. Apparently, ideology has no place in the delicate rhythms of healing.

Doctors' orders and abstract rules—such as "Get plenty of rest" or "Take daily walks"—offer helpful guidelines, but they cannot tell me when I need to change the rules; only my body can do that. That is why so many sick people come to rely upon their bodies for guidance. When Max Lerner was sick with cancer and trying to decide whether to undergo chemotherapy, he went home for a week to consult his "innermost oracle"—his body. "I recalled," he wrote, "how often I had told my seminar students to 'follow the organism.' Now I was doing that."[7]

When I was very weak and spending most of my time in bed, I used to twist and turn, stretching myself into odd positions until I found the one that was just right: curled up in a ball, arching back like a tree in high wind, or belly-up like a cat in the heat of summer. One night I dreamed that I was learning secret yoga positions reserved for the sick and dying to help them make the difficult transitions required by their stations in life; when I woke up, I realized that my body had been teaching me those poses for quite some time. This body-based learning and healing goes on all the time, but usually below the threshold of our conscious awareness; it takes an illness to draw our attention to the marvelously subtle and complex ways our bodies register changes and respond accordingly to protect the integrity of the whole.

I am often reminded that my body knows more than I do, that it has already picked up a disturbance and reacted appropriately before I realize anything is going on. For example, there have been times when I have suddenly, inexplicably, lost interest in sex, only to learn later that I am fighting an infection and need to conserve my resources, or that I am enmeshed in my relationship and need more separateness, or that I am still mad about what happened last week. Not only do our bodies know more; they also cannot lie, much to our occasional embarrassment. I have never been able to keep my voice from cracking when I am on the edge of tears, my face from flushing when a friend teases me about sex, or my hands from shaking when I am nervous. At times like this I try to remind myself: "Your body knows best. Trust it."

There are other times when it appears that my body does not know best, when I reach for that piece of chocolate cake that will make me sicker, rage at loved ones who do not deserve it, or find myself hopelessly attracted to someone I know to be cruel. Like everything that belongs to nature, our bodies have their own inexplicable streaks of madness, the uncontrollable impulses and funny quirks that save us from perfection. They are decidedly multifaceted and pluralistic, as if inhabited by many people, critters, demons, and demigods, as the ancients believed; like the ever-changing currents of water and weather, they resist our domination and persist in leading us into mystery.

In recent years, since I have remembered being molested as an infant, I have come to realize that some of these "crazy" impulses were speaking for, and leading me to, a tortured part of myself I did not know existed. While I saw myself as a relatively happy, healthy, and confident person, my body often told another story, in the timid tilt of my head, the suspicious squint of my right eye, my sudden panics and midnight coughing fits—most of which have increased in recent years. It is as if some encompassing intelligence of body and soul were drawing old wounds to the surface, like a poultice, to bleed openly; perhaps it is in the nature of buried memories to rise again with time, like bodies in a river or rocks in a farmer's field. The recovery of these memories in recent years has taught me a good deal about the consciousness that resides in my body and the way it protects and maintains the wholeness of my being.

My memories of abuse have come in two forms. Some come as images that flash before me like the clips of a silent movie; they are devoid of feeling and sensation, viewed with an indifferent eye from the ceiling. For example, I watched a man play with what appeared to be a lifeless rag doll, teasing and squeezing her, twisting and turning her, even throwing her against the wall; it was some time before I realized that the rag doll in these pictures was me. The other memories came through my body, often triggered by physical experiences like lovemaking or nausea; they are urgent and chaotic, fraught with fear, pain, and shame. I simply become that one-year-old and feel the shooting pain in my hip as my leg is twisted back, the press of the pillow on my face, the stickiness of semen all over me. There are only physical sensations, no sounds or visuals, no words or faces, as is often the case with preverbal memories. I cannot talk during these episodes, as I could not then; I cry and wave my arms in front of me the way babies do.

These memories pop open in my body like air bubbles surfacing from the deep, perfectly preserved, untouched by conscious recall, as if they had been frozen in ice for a very long time. They could be called "fossil memories," as Oliver Sacks has suggested, since each is "like a still photo preserved from the past—an image which can no longer be integrated into the normal, ever-changing, dynamic, body-image, but has been marooned . . . in an unnatural and strange fixity."[8] Fossil memories often present themselves as neuroses and physical symptoms. As I understand it, our task is to gradually reintegrate these isolated, frozen fragments of memory and bring them into the present, into our understanding of self and world. This is the work of therapy; it is also, I suspect, one of the labors of illness, and it is not an easy task.

As my body was "thawing" during the worst years of my illness, it felt like a soggy field dotted with land mines buried and abandoned in some long-forgotten war. I was often afraid to take a step, to make love, or get a massage, for fear of detonating another memory. I am still shocked and horrified, even disgusted, by the pain that is embedded in my flesh; I have dreamed more than once of discovering the bloody, mangled corpse of a little girl hidden in the woodwork of my house. In one of those dreams I considered stuffing her back into the woodwork; truly, I am a reluctant witness. I find it so difficult to integrate these terrifying possibilities into my everyday awareness that I often slip into disbelief, convincing myself that I am making it all up.

Sometimes I hate my body for making me remember, for simply being that vulnerable and wounded. I prefer to identify with that detached omniscient eye on the ceiling, rather than assume the messy, bloody, provoking truth of my body. But my body won't let me tear myself in two like that anymore. Like many survivors of sexual abuse, I feel thankful that my body allowed me to escape and forget for so long, only to wonder why she has reeled me back in—now—to remember and re-collect the scattered parts of my self and my history.

BODY AND PSYCHE, SYMPTOMS AND SOLUTIONS

I cannot separate my current illness from my recovery from sexual abuse; they have occurred simultaneously in my life, and the symptoms and symbols of each are intermingled in my psyche and dreams. During my first winter with CFIDS, I dreamed repeatedly that my house was being invaded by malevolent forces, images that accurately described: (1) my molestation experiences, (2) my process of memory recall, in which the ego defenses that originally buried the memories were broken down to admit the awful truth, and (3) the mechanics of my disease, which so undermined my immunity that I was unable to cope with the invasion of microbal intruders: viruses, mold spores, pollen, and the like. All three processes share the imagery of boundary violation.

I make these connections with some trepidation, because many people have suggested that CFIDS is not a real disease but a mental disorder, a "psychoneurotic condition," as Stephen Strauss, the first researcher to study CFIDS at the National Institutes of Health, once stated—despite the presence of painful and debilitating physical symptoms. Statements like these reflect, more than anything else, the bafflement and helplessness of the scientific community in the face of the CFIDS epidemic; as Susan Sontag observed in her historical study of social attitudes toward disease, "Theories that diseases are caused by mental states . . . are always an index of how much is not understood about the physical terrain of a disease."[9]

Anyone who has lived with an illness that eludes medical identification can attest that friends, family, and physicians are often quick to recommend psychiatrists and dismiss complaints as hypochondria—until a diagnosis is finally made. That is why so many sick people are relieved, even elated, to receive a diagnosis, even though the news is rarely good.

Until the mechanics of a disease are understood, theories of mental origin circulate in the popular mind, and the consequences of those notions are devastating to those afflicted. Patients are often viewed as morally deficient or psychologically damaged, symptoms are not taken seriously, medical and legal claims are denied, and employment opportunities are limited.[10] As a result, there are many people living with disabling diseases who have lost the support of family and friends, been unable to find a physician to care for them, and, though not able to work, cannot qualify for disability insurance. The suggestion that we have created our illnesses out of our own neuroses is an added and intolerable cruelty, especially given the social stigma that surrounds mental illness in our society. No wonder many people with CFIDS have responded to this assault of public ignorance and prejudice by insisting that CFIDS is strictly an organic syndrome with no psychological basis.

It appears to me that both sides of the controversy are struggling over a false dichotomy that we Americans of European descent inherited from the Scientific Revolution: that body and mind are separate and related only by cause and effect. In that paradigm illnesses are either physical or mental in origin, and the line between the two makes a big difference in the lives of sick people; for patients with maladies deemed organic are treated respectfully, and those with so-called mental problems are dismissed with derision. But the experience of illness defies that dichotomy, insisting that body and psyche are inseparable. One does not come before the other; rather they reflect each other, as anyone who has experienced the depression that accompanies low blood sugar, lack of sleep, or the flu can verify. Susan Griffin, who has lived with CFIDS for several years, explained, "At one point I saw that my physical illness and my despair were not separate. This is not to deny the physical. It's not to say that my mental condition causes my illness. That's like saying my hand causes my fingers! What I mean is body and psyche are one. You experience them all at once."[11]

Since illnesses are experienced in the dimensions of both body and psyche, their cures do best to draw upon the information and resources of both. It is very important for the medical community to pursue the organic basis for CFIDS and other diseases that are not understood or able to be treated at this time, but it is also important that those who are living with baffling illnesses give their whole stories, not just the test results, but their thoughts and feelings, dreams and histories, for we also need that information in order to understand these diseases fully. I remember the day I mentioned to my doctor, as an aside, that I had been depressed for months; she stopped, stared at me for a moment, and exclaimed, "Why didn't you tell me?" Apparently, severe depression can be a symptom of allergic response, chemical sensitivity, or an imbalance of neuro-transmitters, all of which are common occurrences with CFIDS and can be treated. "Please," my doctor continued, "tell me all your symptoms, not just the physical ones, but the mental and emotional ones too."

When body and soul were divorced from each other in the European imagination during the seventeenth century, physical processes were described as mechanical operations, and psychic processes were denied as figments of the imagination which only the weak, stupid, or sick would take seriously. These assumptions color our attitudes to this day, despite the wealth of clinical experience and medical research that demonstrates a body-mind unity. Since I have been sick, I have learned with the help of my doctor to take the seemingly imaginary symptoms—the depression, fears, nightmares, body memories, confusion, and disorientation—as seriously as the apparently physical ones. I have also learned, with the help of my dreams, that this illness is facilitating my recovery from childhood sexual abuse by taking me to deeper layers of my body memory, activating a cellular consciousness that remembers not only what has happened, but how to heal.

I had a dream the night before I received my CFIDS diagnosis and learned there was no cure for it; the dream showed me how my incest recovery would continue through the agency of my illness. In that dream I belonged to a group of women incest survivors who met weekly to blaze trails through rough wooded territory. We hung little mirrors from the branches of trees to see better and tried very hard to do it right; even so, we kept getting lost, confused, and separated, and ended up fighting among ourselves. Finally we stopped and asked ourselves: How can we keep from "losing it" like this, from dissociating and splitting apart? As soon as we asked the question, a wise woman appeared and demonstrated a simple spiritual exercise for pulling ourselves back together and cultivating the self-possession of the masters: to collapse with exhaustion. We proceeded to do exactly that, each one of us dropping to the floor with a loud sigh, then, one by one, we told the stories of our lives, our deepest hurts, regrets, and yearnings. As we connected with ourselves and each other, a deep calm enveloped and united us.

Exhaustion is the hallmark of CFIDS, and I collapse with it several times a day—in my car at stoplights, in a chair at the doctor's office, on tiny patches of grass between stores, and at home on the couch, on the floor, in the tub, in my bed. My dream seemed to be saying that one of the strongest symptoms of my disease—exhaustion—offered a much-needed solution to the quandaries of my life, in the unfathomable wisdom of the body. It taught me a healthy respect for physical symptoms and what they require of us.

Symptoms crack through the hardened facades of "health," that mesh of habitual attitudes, assumptions, and successful behaviors that can so easily steer us off course from ourselves. Like all intense physical sensations, whether painful or pleasurable, they force the mind back toward feeling and the visceral truths of our immediate experience. When I am bone tired, I cannot pretend to be happy or gracious, nor can I pass as perfectly competent; I am what I am and that is all there is. As a result, the ongoing exhaustion of my illness has slowly undermined my "good girl" persona and perfectionist habits I had learned as a child to steer my way through the land mines of adult psyches, and it has cultivated in me a self-attentiveness I now need in order to survive. I could not say that I have the self-possession of a master, as my dream promised, but I do have the ability to pause and check in with myself while collapsed, and the license to say no to the things I do not want to do, and yes to that which I must do for the survival of my body and soul.

Sometimes I think we would lose ourselves altogether if it were not for our stubborn, irrepressible symptoms, calling us, requiring us, to re-collect ourselves and reorient ourselves to life. The longer I am sick the more I realize that illness is to health what dreams are to waking life—the reminder of what is forgotten, the bigger picture working toward resolution. If I were to name that intelligence, that deep knowing which operates through the agency of our dreams and flesh, I would call it soul, agreeing with philosopher Morris Berman, who once said: "Soul is another name for what the body does."[12]

3

TOXIC HEALTH: CULTURAL ASSUMPTIONS AND ILLUSIONS

We cannot understand the body completely without taking history and culture into account. . . . The lonely individual suffering from the uncanny power of some strange ailment should realize that he is troubled in part by the unlived life of a collective which has dreamed his body process into being.

—Arnold Mindell[1]

When I first got sick with CFIDS, I held many beliefs about health and illness that proved to be useless at best and harmful at worst. A lifetime of relative ease and full activity, assisted by the periodic intervention of miracle drugs, had taught me to assume health; illnesses, I thought, were just small bumps in the road of life, temporary breakdowns in the well-oiled machinery of my body, that could—and should—be quickly remedied, preferably without making a complaint or skipping a day of work. Like many informed Americans, I did all the "right" things to ensure a long and healthy life; I exercised regularly, ate whole grains and organic vegetables (although I did indulge in many a bowl of Häagen-Dazs coffee ice cream), avoided tobacco and alcohol, and cultivated a close circle of loved ones. I was pleased and proud to check "very good" for my health on job applications.

I was shocked, then, to find myself gravely ill at thirty-six for no apparent reason; in fact, I ignored and minimized my developing symptoms—the fevers, tiredness, muscle aches, and general ennui—for quite some time, and so precipitated my eventual collapse.

Once I finally admitted to being seriously sick—when I could barely stand up—I was again surprised to learn that no one really knows what CFIDS is or how to help someone who suffers from it. My regular doctor, herbalist, and acupuncturist all shook their heads, baffled. With a desperation familiar to many sick people, I tried all manner of diets, remedies, and visualizations, searching for a cure without success; in the process I wasted a great deal of time, energy, and money, which would have been better spent learning how to live with CFIDS, rather than attempting to escape it. As the illness wore on, I struggled against the limitations it imposed, out of an old, ingrained habit of pushing limits and overcoming weariness to fulfill my ambitions and responsibilities—only to make myself sicker, over and over again. And despite my best efforts to affirm myself, and wonderfully supportive dreams and friends, I felt ashamed of myself for getting sick—and staying sick.

With all this in mind, I had to ask myself: How have I come to be so ill-equipped to face illness, to accept and abide by the requirements of my body? That question has prompted me to examine the cultural values, attitudes, and assumptions that surround health and shape our experience of illness in this society, and the WASP culture of my upbringing in particular. I began to collect articles and books on the subject, filling my shelves with everything from Garrison Keillor's *Lake Wobegon Days* to the classic anthropology text *Magic, Witchcraft, and Curing* by John Middleton, and, slowly, a few answers began to emerge.

I learned that every culture has its own definitions and explanations of health and disease that are informed by a shared world view.[2] An allopathic, or Western, doctor, trained in the scientific paradigm that focuses upon physical cause and effect, will look for a physical cause in illness and seek to control it with mechanical interventions, such as drugs or surgery. A Chinese acupuncturist, on the other hand, working from a philosophy of balance and harmony, will look for an underlying imbalance of energies in the body and help the patient reestablish balance with needle treatments, diet, and life-style changes. And a Peruvian shaman, who relates to powers of an invisible world that borders on the visible, might identify witchcraft as the cause of a lingering illness and perform a ritual to lift the curse, so that the body can heal of its own accord. And all three effect cures.

I suspect that these wildly divergent understandings of illness are simply taking different slants on the same phenomenon, by focusing upon different factors involved. It is like taking three people to view a landscape and asking them what they see. One sees a deer at the edge of the forest, another comments on the interplay of colors in the scene as a whole, while the third might see a bear in the outline of a hilltop. So, greatly simplified, doctors focus upon the physical disease process, acupuncturists study the energetics of health, and shamans address the bigger question of why this person got sick and not another.

Of course, many doctors would readily dismiss the works of an acupuncturist or shaman as ignorant superstition or quackery, but that unwillingness to consider the evidence simply reflects their immersion in the scientific worldview of their training, which, by the way, we share as patients and members of what is commonly called the modern world, that is, the last eight hundred years of white, Euro-American civilization. These agreed-upon assumptions, or hidden ideologies, comprise what some observers have termed a "cultural trance." When such a trance is operating, shared assumptions are experienced as literal facts or absolute truth, and all evidence to the contrary is quickly dismissed as untrue because it's threatening, as

Galileo discovered when he dared to suggest that the earth was round, not flat. A serious illness, especially one that cannot be readily explained or remedied within a given worldview, poses such a threat; it cracks the cultural trance and reveals the limitations of those shared assumptions we take for granted.

IDEALS OF HEALTH AND FEARS OF ILLNESS

The entire discussion of health and disease in the modern world of Western medicine is couched in militaristic metaphors of attack, invasion, and defense. Disease is treated like a foreign enemy—something that must be vigilantly avoided, contained, and eradicated if necessary. In turn, healing is not something the body does for itself, but something that must be done to it as we lie perfectly still. Our bodies are the battlegrounds in this unnamed war, and the weapons of choice in allopathic medicine—drugs and surgery—do not wave the flag of truce or fire occasional shots of warning; they drop bombs, often destroying all that surrounds as well.

Allopathic (meaning "against suffering") medicine and psychology take an aggressive stance against disease with the explicit aim of eliminating pain, illness, and infirmity from our world and lives. This is a heroic ideal. It is infused with notions of superiority, expectations of conflict and conquest, that reflect the imperialistic ethos of our culture.

This is not to deny that Western medicine (which several observers now term "cosmopolitan medicine" because it has been extended around the globe with the spread of imperialism) has made some remarkable achievements; I count myself as one of many who would not be alive today without it. It is very good at short-circuiting the disease process in acute episodes, as anyone who has taken antibiotics for a bad infection or undergone emergency surgery can attest, and it's remarkably effective at prolonging life. The development of vaccines, along with improved nutrition, hygiene, and sanitation, has largely eliminated from the industrialized world the infectious diseases that plagued previous generations. Even though other epidemics, like cancer and AIDS, have taken their places, these remarkable successes fueled the fantasy, which has gained popularity since World War II, that we can and will someday control the autonomous life of the body and overcome illness altogether, to feel good, live forever, and never be tired again, as our self-help books proclaim. These are the dreams, utopian ideals, of a privileged people with access to miracle drugs and modes of power that keep many forms of human suffering, and the accompanying feelings of fear, vulnerability, and helplessness, at bay.

These dreams may sustain the well, but they fail the sick, especially those with chronic, debilitating illnesses. When pain and disability prove to be intractable, and savings disappear, marriages flounder, and confidence is shattered, the old answers just do not work anymore. We feel betrayed by the promises of cures that can be found in almost every magazine, and forsaken by doctors, family, and friends who cannot really help, but keep suggesting another treatment. A man with debilitating diabetes finally told his doctor, "In the long run, I'll go down this road myself. Neither you nor anyone else can prevent it or control it or understand it for me."[3] In such cases, both patient and doctor are haunted by unanswered questions, the uneasy ambiguity of mystery, and the rank injustice of suffering.

One of the most difficult things that sick and disabled people encounter is the uncomfortability that many well and able-bodied people feel in the face of infirmity. I have felt that uncomfortability when faced with people who are disfigured or disabled in ways that I am not, confined to a wheelchair or missing a breast or tongue as a result of cancer surgery. I get nervous and worry about saying or doing the wrong thing, remembering the time I squeezed the hand of a friend with arthritis in a gesture of affection, only to see her wince with pain. But beneath that superficial nervousness is a more visceral anxiety that makes me sweat: a deep resistance to those who are so obviously marked and limited by their fates. I have caught myself cataloguing the differences between us in my mind, as if the simple acknowledgment of our commonality would enable their disasters somehow to infect me and spoil that slim vestige of health and hope I cling to in my own corner of misery.

I dread having to tell people I am sick, or still sick, because many respond with theories about what I did to make myself sick or suggestions of what I could do to get well—both of which just make me feel worse for being sick. I remember one very difficult day when I had two such encounters at the post office. I had just squatted down to get my mail from our box, and discovered that I did not have the strength to stand up, when an acquaintance I had not seen in more than a year approached and asked how I was doing. I put on a brave front, refusing to explain why I was sitting, cross-legged, on the floor of the post office, and told her I was basically okay, but had developed CFIDS in the past year; she responded immediately by saying, "I've always thought you work too hard." I stared up at her for a few long seconds, and then held out my hand and asked, "Can you help me up?" Then, as I was heading out the door, weaving a little from dizziness and worried that I would not make it to my car, another acquaintance came running up to me, shouting, "Kat! I hear you have that Epstein-Barr virus. There's this clinic in Mexico I've got to tell you about. They flush your system with hydrogen peroxide and. . . ."

I have come to realize that many people are deeply disturbed by the fact of my continuing illness; they want to help but also need to reassure themselves that disasters like disease can be avoided and, if necessary, easily remedied. Treya Killam Wilber remembered devising theories to explain her mother's colon cancer, only to realize later, when she herself developed cancer, that "it was really fear—unacknowledged, hidden fear—that motivated me to believe the universe made sense and that its forces were more or less within my control. In such a reasonable universe, staying healthy would be a simple matter of avoiding stress or changing my personality or becoming a vegetarian."[4] It's hard to swallow the fact that we have little or no say over the extent and timing or our illnesses.

Before the advent of modern medicine, people gave thanks for good health, counting it as an unexpected blessing, as many traditional peoples still do today. (Remember when people simply wished for good health in the New Year?) Buddhist scriptures taught that the bodies we inhabit are fertile ground for all manner of misfortunes, and no sensible person would entertain expectations of well-being unless they were mad. Well, we must be mad, for now we've come to assume well-being and regard illness as a temporary breakdown of normal "perfect" health.

Our concepts of physical and psychological health have become one-sidedly identified with the heroic qualities most valued in our culture: youth, activity, productivity, independence, strength, confidence, and optimism. Advertisements reflect our picture of health as young, white, slim, athletic . . . and beaming with "the cheerful effervescence of a Bernie Siegel or a Louise Hay," as writer Daniel Harris wryly observed.[5] Even sick people are encouraged to cheer up and be brave, and those who can joke in the midst of obvious agony are revered by all. When we want to describe how healthy an old man is, we say he is "still going strong" or "keeping himself busy." We might say he is in "perfect health." The very coupling of these two words betrays the idealism and striving perfectionism of health in our culture. A small sniffle or a week in the doldrums, not to mention an outbreak of cancer, can spoil that perfection. Health has become an impossible ideal.

Even though we have come to equate perfection with normalcy, imperfection is more often the rule. There is not one of us without some abnormality—flat feet, farsightedness, dyslexia, a heart murmur, an enlarged liver from a bout of hepatitis, or slight brain damage from a fall. Myths, fairy tales, and great works of literature, which abound with cripples and hunchbacks, one-eyed monsters and big-nosed lovers, suggest that these abnormalities are not only normal but somehow necessary in the plot of life; they shape our characters and destinies, forge our greatnesses and smallnesses, while entertaining and instructing others at the same time. However, that sensibility has been lost in recent years, as an increasing number of "abnormalities"—from small breasts to the desire to help others—are labeled as defects or diseases that must be treated, corrected, or overcome. As Jungian analyst Adolf Guggenbuhl-Craig observed, "Once a person went through life with a melancholic temperament; today the same person has to swallow strong medication until he becomes relaxed and stupidly happy."[6] People go jogging three months after a coronary, undergo surgery to correct upturned noses, starve themselves to lose weight, and take workshops to overcome fear, risking health and wealth to attain some mythical ideal of the norm.

Sickness, by these definitions, is not only a breakdown of normal health but a personal failure, which explains why many sick people feel so guilty and ashamed—or angry at anyone who intimates they have done something wrong. Mary Winfrey Trautmann, who wrote of her daughter's struggle with leukemia, observed, "As long as the blood counts are good or within the acceptable range, she will be praised; if they deteriorate, she can expect disapproval from both nurses and doctors; relapse must mean the height of failure then."[7] When symptoms persist and illness becomes chronic, we often find fault with the victim; we call it a lack of will power, a desire for attention, an unwillingness to work or change, rather than question the hidden assumption that it is within our power as human beings to overcome sickness and, in fact, it is our job to do so. Adolf Guggenbuhl-Craig has termed this tendency to accept people only when they get better, heal, or want to heal, "wholeness moralism."

In our infatuation with health and wholeness, illness is one-sidedly identified with the culturally devalued qualities of quiet, introspection, weakness, withdrawal, vulnerability, dependence, self-doubt, and depression. If somebody displays any of these qualities to a great extent, he or she is likely to be considered ill and encouraged to see a doctor or therapist. In a perversion of recent discoveries of body-mind unity, self-help books encourage sick people to cultivate positive attitudes—faith, hope, laughter, self-love, and a fighting spirit—to overcome their diseases. As a result, many sick people are shamed by friends, family, or even their healers into thinking they are sick because they lack these "healthy" attitudes, even though illnesses often accompany critical turning points in our lives, when it is necessary to withdraw, reflect, sorrow, and surrender, in order to make needed changes. Normal life passages, such as birth, adolescence, the crises of middle age, old age, and death, are now treated as illnesses in need of medical intervention, simply because they are often characterized by pain, withdrawal, introspection, and alienation.

"In health," wrote Virginia Woolf, "the general pretence must be kept up and the effort renewed—to communicate, to civilize, to share, to cultivate the desert, educate the native, to work together by day and by night to sport. In illness this make-believe ceases. . . . We cease to be soldiers in the army of the upright; we become deserters. They march to battle. We float with the sticks on the stream; helter-skelter with the dead leaves on the lawn, irresponsible and disinterested and able, perhaps for the first time for years, to look round, to look up—to look, for example, at the sky."[8] As Woolf intimates, the withdrawal, inactivity, and alienation of illness threaten the social order, undermining the faith, optimism, attachments, and obligations that keep systems in power—in the family, workplace, and society at large. In the quiet stillness of the sickbed, where we look up and around, rather than straight ahead, another—truly revolutionary—perspective emerges.

When I'm well, I tend to fill my days with a multitude of meaningful activities—my counseling practice, my writing, a lover, friends and godchildren, political involvements and spiritual practices; but when I get sick, even with minor ailments, I lose my motivation. After six months with CFIDS, I could not remember why I had ever wanted to hike those trails, teach those classes, or attend those meetings. Nothing seemed worth doing—and that awareness shimmered with power. I remember the exact time and place I first realized its enormity; I was sitting on the living-room couch after a long, tiring morning of work, holding a small bowl of rice in my hands. The phone rang, and—quite out of character—I just sat there and let it ring, as I turned the bowl in my hands and admired its perfect shape. I felt privy to one of the world's great secrets: that what *is* is enough, that each moment contains, like the circle of that bowl, the whole of creation in the space it offers, and we need not go anywhere or do anything to find it. Since then there have been times when I have cried bitterly over the losses wrought by my illness, but more often than not I have cherished the serenity of being still and feeling full with the moment at hand, of not wanting anything more than I already have.

Even at my sickest, when I was spending the majority of the daylight hours in bed aching, I knew my illness was showing me facets of truth that I had missed—we had all missed, it seemed—and desperately needed. I did not want a quick cure that would tear me from those insights, though I could not admit that to most friends who wished me a speedy recovery; I wanted to find a way to carry my sickbed revelations back with me into health, to balance the lopsided optimism, confidence, and activity of my earlier life.

The extraordinary technology and powers of intervention that characterize modern medicine can eliminate many devastating symptoms in a flash, but they can also short-circuit a complicated system of suffering and meaning that is instrumental to life and consciousness. Oliver Sacks reported in an article for the *New York Review of Books* that he once cured a brilliant mathematician of migraines, only to discover that the man could no longer do his work. He wrote: "Along with the pathology, the creativity also disappeared, and this made it clear that one has to inspect the economy of the person. . . . It is not sufficient just to make a diagnosis of migraine and give a pill. One has to inquire into the entire human drama that surrounds" an illness.[9]

When problems are quickly solved and we return to our old selves, the questions illnesses inevitably raise—and the insights and opportunities they offer—are erased and nullified. We have developed so many tools, from visualizations to painkillers, for suppressing symptoms and their accompanying question marks that we have lost the ability to come to terms with pain and suffering, to be changed, informed, and even illumined by their presence in our lives.

SYMPTOMS, STORIES, AND THE GRASP OF THE UNKNOWABLE

There is an untold story behind every symptom, an entire human drama surrounding every illness, and only the person who is sick can find and tell that story. Terry Tempest Williams has written of finding the story behind the cancer in her family. Her mother, grandmothers, and six aunts have all had mastectomies, and seven died from cancer; as she put it, "I belong to a Clan of One-Breasted Women." One day, quite by happenstance, she told her father of a recurring dream she has had since childhood. It was of an enormous, blinding flash of light in the desert at night that illuminated the buttes and mesas and permeated her being. Her father proceeded to tell her that when she was a baby the entire family had witnessed an atomic explosion, part of a program of aboveground atomic testing, when driving through the desert of Nevada in 1957.

"It was at that moment," wrote Tempest Williams, "I realized the deceit I had been living under. Children growing up in the American Southwest, drinking contaminated milk from contaminated cows, even from the contaminated breasts of their mothers, my mother—members, years later, of the Clan of One-Breasted Women." With that realization has come the decision to "question everything," and the commitment to protest atomic testing through writing and acts of civil disobedience. "Tolerating blind obedience in the name of patriotism or religion," warns Tempest Williams, "ultimately takes our lives."[10]

Jungian analyst Albert Kreinheder, who wrote of his experiences with cancer, arthritis, and tuberculosis, described his process of finding the "image behind the symptom" when he started having chest pain. He worried for weeks that he might get tuberculosis, and die from it, as his mother had years before; then a sputum analysis revealed that, in fact, he had active tuberculosis. After some reflection, Kreinheder realized that he had an unconscious identification with his mother—the visceral sense that his body was his mother, and not just his mother, but the mother goddess herself—and concluded that he had the chest pain because he was on bad terms with her.

In response to that realization, Kreinheder taught himself to pray to the mother goddess, which was not an easy task, as he had to overcome his own skepticism and anti-mother sentiments. Through his prayers, however, he came to feel the goddess in his body as a gentle soothing energy that seemed incompatible with illness. Even though the TB never went away altogether, Kreinheder felt redeemed by the encounter, "healed to a wholeness far beyond my previous so-called health."[11]

The stories Tempest Williams and Kreinheder tell remind us of how much we have to learn, as individuals and as societies, from our illnesses and the sacred spaces we inhabit in pain. (When my lover's father was dying of cancer, he bemoaned the fact that he would never teach again, saying, "I have so much more to teach now.") Cosmopolitan medicine banishes that knowledge by insisting that suffering is without meaning, and unnecessary, because pain can be technically eliminated. Symptoms are divorced from the person who has them and the situations that surround them, secularized as mechanical mishaps, and so stripped of their stories, the spiritual ramifications and missing pieces of history that make meaning.

As a result, sick people and the ones who love them are left to rage at the utter meaningless of their suffering; many have told me that this is the most difficult aspect of illness to endure. In our attempt to banish illnesses from our world, we banish the knowledge that can save us—whether it is the understanding that radiation kills or the recognition that the great mother demands our attention—and commit the sick to suffer the added burden of meaninglessness and irrelevance.

Traditional peoples, who have always lived with illness and infirmity, teach ways to endure pain, understand sickness, and relate to those who are afflicted, enabling everyone—the sick and the well, the young and the old—to derive meaning from the lifelong encounter with death. Traditional Cherokee, for example, understand sickness to be a purifying experience intended to return us to our path of destiny and of spirit.[12] The sick person and his or her relations perform time-honored rituals to clear their hearts and facilitate that purification. In shamanic traditions like this, which are the oldest and most universal means of healing in the world, illness is assumed to have spiritual dimensions; no shaman attempts to cure without first invoking the gods. As the God of Deuteronomy declared: "I wound and I heal; there is no rescue from my grasp."

In the secular world of modern medicine, we try desperately to rescue ourselves from the grasp of the Unknowable. Doctors have supplanted the gods, deciding when life begins and ends, working miracles, and taking the credit for their successes. This aura of divinity that surrounds the medical profession in our society, and the extraordinary expectations that come with it, is the source of much pain and frustration for doctor and patient alike, especially when cures are not forthcoming. Nancy Mairs, who has had multiple sclerosis since adolescence, defined the situation well in her essay "On Being a Cripple":

> The absence of a cure often makes MS patients bitter towards their doctors. Doctors are, after all, the priests of modern society, the shamans, whose business is to heal, and many an MS patient roves from one to another, searching for the "good" doctor who will make him well. Doctors too think of themselves as healers, and for this reason many have trouble dealing with MS patients, whose disease in its intransigence defeats their aims and mocks their skills. . . . I have always tried to be gentle with my doctors, who often have more at stake in terms of ego than I do. I may be frustrated, maddened, depressed by the incurability of my disease, but I am not diminished by it, and they are.[13]

The sense of diminishment we so often experience in the grasp of the Unknowable, the face of the incurable, probably has something to offer us from a spiritual perspective, but in the secular world of twentieth-century America, it is without meaning and so intolerable. That is why the first commandment in illness is to get well. Sick people are under tremendous pressure, from themselves and from others, to overcome their ailments and return to life as usual in our fast-paced, production-oriented world. We feel obligated to our doctors, employers, and family members to seek medical advice, follow doctor's orders, and discontinue any personal practices considered unhealthy, from smoking to eating potato chips. Sick or not, we run, swim, bike, and hike, eat bran muffins, yogurt, and salads, take vitamins and medicines, floss our teeth, examine our breasts, and scrutinize our moles in a desperate and dutiful dash to maintain our increasingly precarious health. Americans spend more time and money on health care than ever before, while at the same time, more and more people suffer from chronic, debilitating illnesses, such as diabetes, arthritis, heart disease, and immune disorders. The U.S. medical-industrial complex is second in size only to the military-industrial complex—and still it is failing.

Government-funded research focuses upon the search for medical cures rather than prevention. Even when prevention is discussed, it is only in terms of things the individual can do, such as quit smoking or reduce fat consumption, and not in terms of what our society could do, such as reduce pollution or provide quality food and prenatal care; for actual prevention would require changing the basic institutions of our society. In our collective denial we have turned health into a personal responsibility rather than a social concern; we diagnose many of our difficulties coping with a sick society and a toxic environment as individual health problems. In fact, we use medical diagnosis to cover up social problems, as scientist Fritjof Capra noted, "We prefer to talk about our children's 'hyperactivity' or 'learning disability,' rather than examine the inadequacy of our schools; we prefer to be told we suffer from 'hypertension' rather than change our overcompetitive business world; we accept ever-increasing rates of cancer rather than investigate how the chemical industry poisons our food to increase profits."[14] Truly, we live in a sick society.

A HISTORICAL PERSPECTIVE

How is it that we have gone so awry? I find it useful to look back to the time when our modern age was born, with the rise of capitalism and the Scientific Revolution of sixteenth- and seventeenth-century Europe. The tensions and conflicts of that time illuminate the hidden ideologies of contemporary medical attitudes and practices.[15]

During the Middle Ages the feudal system and the Catholic Church dominated and restricted the social, economic, and intellectual life to such an extent that revolt was inevitable. That revolt came from the growing merchant class, recently empowered by the flourishing beginnings of capitalism, and manifested in the Protestant Reformation and the Scientific Revolution, which together defined a new paradigm for understanding reality.

In the fifteenth, sixteenth, and seventeenth centuries the capitalist drive for increased productivity fostered technological development, such as the invention of clocks and firearms, earth-altering activities like mining and deforestation, global exploration, and the conquest of new territories and peoples. Science, as we know it today, grew alongside these developments, enabling and justifying them, by formulating a pragmatic, empirical body of knowledge that could be used to dominate and control nature. It may be helpful to realize that Europeans had just endured a few hundred years of continental cooling, advancing glaciers, crop failures, mass starvation, plague, wars, and witch trials, which must have convinced many of nature's "evils": her dark, chaotic, and devouring aspect. Leaders looked for ways to manage the terrifying powers of nature; Sir Francis Bacon, considered to be one of the fathers of modern science, declared, "I come . . . leading to you Nature and all her children to bind her to your service and make her your slave."

With the rise of the scientific paradigm, ancient images of the Earth and the body as alive, infused with divine presence and purpose, were slowly replaced by notions of the Earth as inert matter and nature as chaos that must be controlled and mastered by humankind. René Descartes extended this mechanical worldview to living organisms, further developing what is now called the "Cartesian split" between body and mind, which is so central to the medical practice and popular thinking of our day. Since the body was no longer sacred, autopsies and surgeries were performed for the first time, revealing internal organs; the body was likened to a machine composed of moving parts that follow physical laws of motion like clockwork. The theory of contagion was introduced and attention shifted from the sick person to the mechanics of disease, the breakdown and repair of the "body machine," to use a phrase from Descartes.

The ramifications of these developments are immense. As Jeanne Achterberg explained in her history of women in healing, "When spirit no longer is seen to abide in matter, the reverence for what is physical departs. Hence medicine no longer regarded itself as working in the sacred spaces where fellow humans find themselves in pain and peril, and where transcendence is mostly desired."[16] This secularization of the body and of the experience of illness developed in reaction to the domination of the Catholic Church in medieval times; it was an attempt to carve out some territory beyond the control of the Church, which had shown itself quite capable of excommunicating, imprisoning, and murdering anyone who challenged Church doctrine. Besides, the Church had not offered much help for the sick during the Middle Ages, beyond prayer and the healing miracles of cherished relics; as French historian Jules Michelet explained, "On Sundays, after Mass, the sick came in scores, crying for help—and words were all they got: 'You have sinned, and God is afflicting you. Thank Him; you will suffer so much the less torment in the life to come.' "[17]

In reaction to the Church's otherworldly orientation and distrust of the senses, Galileo, Bacon, and others set forth an empirical method of scientific inquiry which restricted attention to that which can be quantifiably measured—observable phenomena. This move, which philosopher William Barrett termed a "flight from consciousness,"[18] put many cherished medieval notions, from the idea that the earth is flat to the recognition that the earth has a soul, up for critical review. It also excluded subjective, qualitative experience—such as feel, touch, and smell, intuition, dream, and revelation—from the realm of scientific discourse. Even though many of the scientists of the day recognized invisible and divine dimensions of reality, and practiced occult arts such as alchemy and astrology, when the scientific paradigm was fully entrenched during the industrial age, psychic processes were categorically dismissed as imagination or superstition.

So developed the thinking that nothing is real unless it can be physically proven—a notion that has caused considerable anguish for many people with CFIDS and other undiagnosed illnesses whose doctors refuse to believe they are actually sick because researchers have not yet found the tests that can objectively confirm it. When I was getting sick, feeling tired and achy all over, I kept wondering: Is this real, or is it just my imagination?, as if my experience were not real. I was fortunate to find a doctor who not only believed me, but taught me to pay close attention to the sensations in my body, and the subtle shifts of mood and thought that accompanied them, so that we could work together to devise a recovery program—but she is an exception by far.

Finally, Sir Isaac Newton, in his studies of gravity and light, developed the reductionist experimental method still used today; it attempts to understand a whole by examining its parts, asks *how* something works rather than *why* it works, and derives abstract formulas to predict future results. This approach has given us extraordinary insight into the microscopic workings of disease, and the capacity to predict consequences and intervene, but it has also encouraged the fragmentation of contemporary medical specialization and kept the big picture of how living systems function as wholes in reciprocating relationship with the environment out of sight. As a result, physicians now find themselves at a loss to understand, or cure, many of today's major systemic disorders.

While the Scientific Revolution emerged as a revolt against the medieval Church and feudal system, it did continue, and even encourage, a few medieval traditions: the repression of the body, the feminine, and nature itself, and the oppression of women, children, animals, and native peoples. Internal repression and external oppression go hand in hand in any culture of supremacy. Descartes defended vivisection with the explanation that animals do not suffer, that their cries mean nothing more than the creak of a wheel. He also likened feelings to "pets in the house of the master, Reason," which must be subdued along with all other expressions of the autonomous powers of nature. Childbirth and child-rearing practices shifted their focus from offering nurturance to developing mastery and self-control, giving rise to the embattled ego as we know it today. Mental asylums were established for the first time in an attempt to control and eliminate the craziness that was previously understood to be part of life and any community. The notion of progress emerged, replacing ancient and medieval concepts of time as cyclic, to justify and facilitate these dramatic changes.

Before Descartes most healers addressed themselves to the interplay of body and soul, treating patients within the context of physical, social, and spiritual influences. Hippocrates, who is often called the father of Western medicine, taught that the body is capable of healing itself through the "mysterious, divine powers of nature that shaped it," and that it constantly adjusts to changing environmental conditions through ongoing cycles of health and disease. The role of the physician, he explained, was to assist those natural powers by facilitating the disease process that is the healing, and he warned against short-circuiting healing by remedying symptoms.

The traditional folk healers of Western Europe, who were mostly women, employed a variety of tools to address the unique needs of each sick person, invoking deities, examining dreams and omens, giving massages, preparing herbal remedies, prescribing special diets, discussing problems with the family, and performing curing rituals. However, their allegiances with the poor, and popularity among the peasant classes, earned them the wrath of the ruling classes, and most were killed—or driven underground—during the witch hunts of the fourteenth and fifteenth centuries. The male profession of medicine, based in the scientific worldview, rose to take their place.

ILLNESS AS ANTIDOTE

Now, some three hundred years later, we are in a position to see the results and acknowledge the limitations of the scientific ideology that informs modern medical practice and popular notions of health and disease. I would have to agree with Jungian analyst Arnold Mindell, who has worked extensively with sick and dying people, that "a long personal or cultural history that has repressed the pagan gods encourages illness."[19] As many indigenous peoples would explain, when we forget the gods, the gods forget us. If the loop of remembrance that sustains life is broken, things fall apart, wither, and die.

Biologist René Dubos offered a more secular explanation for this dynamic in *Mirage of Health,* noting that all species, including human beings, maintain health through a process of constant adaptation to relatively stable environments. This adaptation, or biological learning, manifests as acquired immunity, physical tastes, and instincts, which one might expect, but also as the cultural customs, taboos, and religious practices that evolve over the course of many generations. Peoples who practice the traditional ways of their ancestors, developed through centuries of adaptation to the landscape, weather, vegetation, animal life, and spirits of a given locale, generally maintain good health. The history of the Navajo demonstrates this point; like many indigenous peoples, they lived according to traditional ways in harmony "with the mountain soil, the pollen of the native plants and all other sacred things" for centuries, suffering no great waves of disease until the white man appeared.[20]

Dubos argued that "Western man" denies the legacy of traditional wisdom in a desire for progress. Natural limits and boundaries are regarded as challenges to overcome; we thrill to the experience of entering new territories—from mountaintops to ocean floors, the inner workings of the human body to the outer reaches of space—and speak of capturing foreign markets like marbles in a game, without attention to the consequences of our actions. We assume change is for the better, constantly moving to new locales, experimenting with synthetic products, unusual diets, alternative life-styles, and improved technologies, all of which disturb the delicate ecological equilibrium that exists within and without our bodies. These changes occur so rapidly that our bodies and cultures do not have time to adapt biologically—if that is possible—inviting danger and new diseases.

Many technologies developed to solve one problem create another, sometimes greater, one, as our experience with asbestos, pesticides, and nuclear power now attests. I have recently learned that my exposure to ink when I worked as a printer during my twenties contributed to the breakdown of immunity that now shows itself in my illness; it never occurred to me or my employer at the time, when my hands were perpetually stained from work, that it could cause such problems in the future. Medical technologies are also prone to unexpected aftereffects; reproductive aids, such as oral contraceptives, the IUD and DES, have caused chronic infections, infertility, cervical cancer, birth defects, and even death. There's a name now for medically induced illnesses—iatrogenesis—and they're increasingly common, since drugs developed to combat one disease often create side effects that breed new diseases.

Antibiotics, for example, alter the normal balance of bacterial flora in the intestines, permitting more resistant organisms to invade and proliferate, as women plagued by vaginal infections can attest. I suspect it is no coincidence that the postwar generation raised on antibiotics is at greater risk of developing immune disorders like AIDS and CFIDS. Our attempts to control beget the uncontrollable, such as proliferating cancer cells and disintegrating immunity, sometimes termed the diseases of civilization. "Like the sorcerer's apprentice," observed Dubos, we have "set in motion forces that are potentially destructive and may someday escape our control."[21]

Carl Jung offered a more psychological explanation for this peculiar failing or vulnerability of white Western civilization: "When the God is not acknowledged, egomania develops, and out of this mania comes sickness."[22] Jung was referring to the secular traditions of European history, spawned by the Scientific Revolution, which effectively banished soul and divinity from our perception of the physical universe, and more intimately, our bodies and the earth itself. As we forgot the sacred dimension of life, we also lost much of our sense of awe, respect, and humility before all things, which normally place restraints upon our so-human tendency to explore, manipulate, and control. So, as Jung explained, egomania develops, a false sense of pride, supremacy, and omnipotence that has led to all manner of excesses during the modern era, including cultural imperialism and ecological devastation; this rampant extraversion has also become our standard for health. According to Jung, it inevitably results in illness, for illness is the antidote.

Recently I spoke with an old friend, a woman I had roomed with several years ago in Texas; she was astounded to hear I had CFIDS, saying: "But you were the healthiest person I've ever known. You biked everywhere, swam every day, ate sprouts and drank herbal teas before anyone else, and lived on a few hours of sleep a night . . . what happened?" I found myself responding, without thinking, "I guess I went so far to one extreme I ended up at the other."

Sometimes I am glad I did so much before getting sick, since I am not sure I will ever get the chance again, but I also wonder whether I may have used up some lifetime allotment of physical reserves, assuming they were unlimited in what now seems to be a gesture of defiance, a maniacal drive for health, purity, and the good life. A friend of mine, who had something like CFIDS several years ago, before there was a name for it, planted that idea in my head one day during the first year of my illness; she stopped by the house on a break between jobs, pulled a chair up to my bed, and said,

"The good news is that you will get better someday. The bad news is that you have used up your life savings of energy, and all you have left is your checking account. Every time you spend energy, you will have to reserve an equal amount in order to keep going."

I was never taught to live my life that way, and I had a hard time seeing it as anything but defeat, until I read the following words from the journal of Audre Lorde, an African-American poet: "Living with cancer has forced me to consciously jettison the myth of omnipotence, of believing—or loosely asserting—that I can do anything."[23] It is that myth of omnipotence, which is such a salient feature of the American spirit it has become the air we breathe without thinking, that is destroyed by the ravages of illness.

The traditions of white Western civilization have taught us to ignore and deny the sensations, instincts, dreams, and revelations our bodies continually generate to maintain a life-sustaining equilibrium. Now that I am sick, I am appalled to think that I used to respond to tiredness by pushing through it like a bulldozer to get my work done, or swim the full mile no matter what. Our determined efforts to pursue abstract goals and ideals, be it success, enlightenment, social responsibility, or even health, lead us dangerously astray, producing an intoxicating high and false pride that immediately collapse under the onslaught of illness. "Insidious thing, pride," wrote Laura Chester during the throes of lupus, "to assume you are better, know better . . . putting down others in order to feel secure, better than, more righteous, but what a fragile security we build for ourselves, out of sticks and straw, like the first and second little pigs."[24]

There is nothing like a serious illness to blow down our fragile houses of sticks and straw. Standing amid the rubble of their lives and thoughts, people with serious illnesses undertake the task of building a new house, a new way of living, one that holds closer to the ground of being, the feedback and teachings of their bodies and souls.

Sick people often speak of having to unlearn the habits of their upbringing in order to live well with their illnesses and heal, if possible. One of the most deeply ingrained cultural imperatives we must confront is the work ethic and its equation of personal worth with productivity. Everyone I know who is sick feels guilty at times for "not doing anything"; it is that guilt that often prompts me to overextend myself. When I showed early drafts of this book to friends who were sick, many responded—much to my horror—with shame, saying, "I didn't do anything when I was sick, and you wrote a book!" I used to have the same reaction whenever I read my college alumni bulletin; while I was in bed, gathering my strength for a trip to the post office, struggling to remember why I needed to go, my classmates were raising children, working at full-time jobs, serving on nonprofit boards, and winning awards!

Dr. Arnold Beisser, who was paralyzed with polio in young adulthood, wrote of having to drop the struggle to "make something of myself and find a place in the world" through "acts of will and effort" and learn to "surrender and accept what I had become" instead.[25] We learn, as Beisser did, to stop comparing ourselves with others, with what we used to be able to do in the past or hope to be able to do in the future, and to simply accept ourselves the way we are. I have noticed that when I can catch myself making those comparisons and stop, I feel a tremendous relief, as if a storm had just veered off to the west, the leaves were settling, and the birds beginning to sing again. Beisser wrote that this simple gesture of self-acceptance made him feel whole for the first time ever, even though he was still bound to his wheelchair.

Illness is the shadow of Western civilization, the antithesis of the rampant extraversion and productivity it so values. As we attempt to exile disease from our world, it persists to haunt us with an ever-menacing guise, and we need it all the more to be whole, to save us from the curse of perfectionism.

So certain realities remain to plague us. The best of people get sick, and many of those who do all the "right" things stay sick or die, while others recover for no apparent reason. Epidemics come and go. As soon as we find the cure for one, another arises. We would like to think we could banish disease with rest, exercise, diet, medicine, prayer, or positive attitudes, but few so-called cures are reliable enough to trust, as anyone who has been sick awhile can tell you. They're just good ways to live, in sickness or health.

4

DANCING WITH DEATH: VEGETATIVE PROCESSES AT WORK

Everyone is pregnant with death. Everyone needs it. Near death we all have the same chance. We all have the chance to become our total selves.

—a thirty-year-old man with AIDS,
after coming out of a coma[1]

Illness is the simple though painful reminder that we are not the masters of our bodies or our lives. So humbled, we find ourselves in the presence of that great Mystery, for lack of a better word, which infuses our flesh, our dreams, and the circumstances of our lives with the hidden purposes of life. Illnesses open us to these hidden mysteries; in fact, many indigenous peoples consider sickness to be one of the most reliable means of revelation and shamanic initiation.

I came down with the flu once as a teenager and spent the afternoon sleeping on the couch. At one point I tried to get up to go to the bathroom, but got so dizzy that I whirled around and fell back down, gulping for air. With each inhalation I felt myself blow up like a balloon, my skin stretching like cellophane over hot bread. Each breath took me higher until I could see my body below me, limp and disheveled. For some reason, I did not panic, but just floated there, like a balloon on a string in midair, for quite a while. Then, slowly deflating with each exhalation, I drifted back into my body.

Not long after that, my English teacher gave us an assignment to write a story about something that had happened to us in our lives. My life seemed endlessly uneventful at the time, so I wrote about this experience of leaving my body and, since that was not long enough, threw in a dream I had had that afternoon of driving over the horizon into clouds that took the shape of a huge thunderbird. My paper came back with a little note attached: "See me after class," ominous words to a student's ears. But when everyone had left, my teacher just handed me a book: a well-worn paperback copy of *Edgar Cayce: The Sleeping Prophet,* and suggested that I might find it interesting. (He also told me not to tell anyone he had given me the book.) That was my introduction to metaphysics, dreams, and the spiritual life; illness was the guide that took me to those gates.

When I first got sick with CFIDS, but did not yet know how serious it was, I dreamed that someone asked me what was wrong and I answered, calmly, "I'm dying." Then the scene switched to my backyard, where beautiful blue morning glories were climbing up into the sky from the roof of my house, and tall, strong cornstalks stood standing to my right. I woke from that dream with a great clarity; I knew I was very sick and had better get help, but more important, I realized that I was in sacred territory, undergoing changes that were so deep and so promising that they could only be likened to dying.

A PRACTICE IN DYING

"A sickbed is a grave," wrote John Donne, who was sick so many times in his life he actually wrote a series of devotions on the subject.[2] Illness is a taste of death, a practice in dying for the living, a visit to the limbos and bardos usually reserved for the nearly or recently deceased. There is the slow grind of discomfort and weakness that dissolves desire. We disengage, like gears unlocking, from participation in the social fabric of life, sinking into a private reality of consuming pain, memory, and shifting awareness that is so remote it is almost impossible to translate it into the terms of everyday consciousness. Grave and mysterious transactions occur in this invisible realm the sick and the dying inhabit, but few remember—or live—to tell of them.

Sometimes there is talk, a sudden urgency, that makes no sense to others; the sick and the dying alike make fervent apologies and stark accusations. When the father of a friend of mine was dying of emphysema, he suddenly opened his eyes one day, fixed them upon the son he had once molested, and whispered: "Let me go. You're my jailer." More often there is no talk, no visible sign of the significant labors of illness; there is just the aloneness, the reverberating isolation of enduring pain and occasional visions that cannot be shared. Even a small sinus infection or a passing flu can sponsor one of those interminable nights of no sleep when we feel the full weight of our existential aloneness. No wonder we fear for our lives when we fall ill, speak of being more dead than alive when we are sick, and of returning from the dead when we get well.

Up until and throughout the Middle Ages, death was understood to be a part of life, not just something that happened at the end of life. A constant companion to the living, death followed one's every footstep like a quiet shadow, sometimes assuming the guise of an enemy brandishing a sword and at other times the face of an ally offering a hand. In the famous dance of death that rose to popularity in fourteenth-century Europe, actors representing everyone from peasant to pope danced through the streets paired with matching corpses bearing their same features and dress, as if to remind onlookers that everybody—rich and poor, noble and ignoble—dance through life with their deaths in arm.

The homeopathic tradition, which grew out of the alchemical experiments of this era, teaches that each person has only one disease in the course of a lifetime; it simply assumes different forms or guises as the various illnesses of one's life and death. Each of our illnesses, then, can be construed as an encounter with that part of ourselves that will most likely someday kill us.

Sick people often describe their illnesses as encounters, struggles, or couplings with the "angel of death." Max Lerner, who survived two kinds of cancer, wrote: "During my illness Death became almost a familiar. . . . In keeping with the Jewish tradition, I veered between I-Thou talks with him and a feeling of awe for the Angel of Death, who is at times one with the Angel of 'God.' "[3] During the first year of my illness, when I secretly felt I was dying, I often likened myself to a seed that was stuck in the ground, unable to sprout and beginning to rot. I knew some great thumb in the sky had pressed me into the cold, dark earth, but I did not know why. Did it intend to bury me for good, or to encourage me to lay roots and find the strength to sprout? Ever since then, whether I am feeling well or sick, I have been conscious of the forces of growth and decay that meet and wrangle in my body, like two straining wrestlers, while the state of my health teeters precariously. When illness strikes, the balance tips, and the powers of decay prevail; cancer cells, viruses, and bacteria proliferate on a physical level, while gloom and despair take over on an emotional level.

The struggle to counter the forces of decay is all-consuming, wearing, and exhausting; no wonder the sick take to bed. After a while death begins to look appealing—not the reality of it so much as the romance of it, the promise of an end to the struggle, and the peace of repose. Since I have been sick, I have occasionally envied people I knew with AIDS or cancer whose deaths appeared to be closer and more assured than mine. I marveled at the ones who fought to live, even on the threshold of death, because I had given up miles back. It was not that I was in so much pain or misery; I had just lost the taste for living. It used to take me hours to get out of bed every morning because I woke feeling so tired and world-weary I could not find a single reason, much less the energy, to mobilize myself. Instead, I dreamed of sinking into the soft, warm dirt of a flower bed, or drifting out to sea on a hazy afternoon. One day, when I found a cat sitting under a tree in the woods, frozen and covered with snow, I thought to myself, What a good way to go.

In this closeness to death sick people often feel the presence of the dead—and their wishes—more keenly. I have repeatedly dreamed of people who have played important roles in my life and since died: my grandmother, an uncle, a favorite teacher, a professional peer who encouraged my work, and others. The dreams often follow a similar format: I start by expressing my gratitude for what they gave me, and they, in turn, remind me of what is most important in life. I feel blessed and inspired by these dream encounters, and so resolved to remember the dead, receive their teachings, and further their efforts. Sometimes, when I take my morning walk, I sense the faint rumbling and murmuring of ancestors in the land, and stop to listen, with my eyes closed. Perhaps it is this affinity with death and the dead that makes so many healthy people afraid of the sick, quick to deny or blame and stay away; they are just making sure they stay on the side of the living.

There are even times when it seems as though sick or dying people derive some supernatural energy from the other side. People often comment on how radiant someone seems after chemotherapy, or the week before dying. I have sometimes felt uplifted and sustained by an energy I could tell was not physical, enabling me to do things, like write for hours on end, that normally I could not do. Occasionally people have noticed and said, "You look great!", which is bewildering to hear when you are very sick. Mary Winfrey Trautmann described this extraordinary energy in her daughter, who was dying of leukemia, as a "burning gemlike flame," explaining that "at the center of her motion lie an expanding consciousness and zest and sensitivity that are immortal."[4]

Death, in its guise as the destroyer, is the active agent in illness. It takes us to our limits, makes us live at the edge, where attention is sharply focused and small things—the smell of perfume or the sound of a saw buzzing down the street—make big differences. It provokes, aggravates, and exacerbates our strengths and weaknesses until something—one's faith in God, an overweaning sense of responsibility, good cheer, or fearlessness—gives way, cut down by the scythe of the Grim Reaper. Every illness, I believe, requires a death, while every healing contains one. We are sometimes diminished, sometimes ennobled, but always transformed, for the Grim Reaper is also the harvester, who cuts back the growth of one year to feed the next.

Several years ago a nine-year-old girl I was coparenting was angry for months, constantly yelling, running off, and slamming doors. We talked about it and tried to arrange solutions for her frustrations, but without much success. Then an interesting thing happened: She got sick with a high fever for a few days, and after that the excess anger was gone, simply gone.

Austrian scientist and philosopher Rudolf Steiner noticed that children often make great leaps in development after an attack of measles or mumps, and went so far as to suggest that childhood diseases help the young to eject unwanted forces of heredity, features of family inheritance that are not suited to their purposes as incoming souls. Steiner opposed the practice of childhood vaccinations, explaining that childhood illnesses are part of a deep-seated growth process beyond our conscious control that should not be prevented.[5] I wonder if the illnesses of adulthood might continue to serve that function of deep-seated growth.

Many Asian and tribal peoples perceive sickness, suffering, and death as manifestations of the body's wisdom, processes of physical and psychic transformation that cleanse us of the bad habits we have accumulated, the everyday neuroses of ordinary consciousness that bind us to suffering and interfere with spiritual growth. John Hobbie, a teacher of the vipassana tradition of Buddhist meditation, who died of an AIDS-related illness in 1989, explained: "Traditional Buddhist teaching suggests that we can be grateful for an affliction, once we have understood that it is the ripening of karma and that its appearance removes the cause. In this understanding, which is a decidedly long-range view, the illness itself is like the 'healing crisis' whose fevers force us to abandon the initial cause of the affliction—which in the Buddhist view is ignorance."[6]

KARMA AND RESPONSIBILITY

I need to digress for a moment and address the question of responsibility in relation to illness, for statements like Hobbie's can be read—through the lens of the Western imagination—to imply that sick people are personally responsible for creating their illnesses through some kind of wrong-thinking or wrong-doing. This notion has caused considerable anguish for people who are sick, as Yaël Bethiem, who lives with ankylosing spondylitis, a disabling immune disorder, described: "One of the hardest parts of this experience has been my constant struggle with the philosophy that we create everything in our lives. It follows, then, since I have not healed, that I have somehow missed the mark. In other words, I have failed. This philosophy . . . has caused my friends to forgo their humanity for the sake of an idea. It has brought me to despair."[7]

I have yet to meet a sick person who has not struggled with

this notion, whether it is dressed in Christian fundamentalism or New Age metaphysics. But the Buddhist concept of ignorance and the ripening of karma is very different from the Christian sense of sin and punishment, as Nan Shin realized in the following story:

After being diagnosed with cancer, Shin read numerous books on the subject and attended a clinic in France for chemotherapy treatments, but all the while she felt "weighted down by . . . some unclear relationship with sickness and death in which guilt and remorse and complicity are involved and it is hard to breathe." Something was "profoundly, powerfully wrong," she wrote in her diary. Then an old friend, who was also a Zen student, visited. He threw his arm around her shoulders and wisecracked, "Good Karma, huh? Brings you close to the Way." Shin wrote later, "The jolt I felt then showed me very clearly that I had been thinking, Bad Karma. Within a fraction of a second the molecules turned themselves round and reorganized. I am flatly grateful to him forever."[8]

At that moment Shin realized that her illness was the cure, not the affliction. Indeed, from a Buddhist perspective, it was an opportunity for enlightenment. This is how John Hobbie could speak of feeling "grateful for an affliction," and Treya Killam Wilber, who lived and died with cancer, could tell a recently diagnosed friend: "Congratulations! You are finally burning off a major chunk of the negative karma that afflicts all of us. We will all have to go through this sooner or later."[9]

It seems to be endemic to the experience of illness to confront body and soul and wonder why it has happened; I suspect that the consideration of guilt and responsibility is part of the process of cleansing and correcting that illness facilitates. Whatever comes up in the asking—whether it is the memory of leaving one's mother to die alone (as it was for May Sarton after her stroke) or the realization that Agent Orange kills (as it was for many Vietnam veterans who have developed cancer)—that is where meaning lies. That is what we must address and redress in some way, with an apology, self-forgiveness, or political action—whatever is called for.

Ultimately, I think the question of responsibility must be answered by each sick person in his or her heart of hearts, amid the anguished turnings of illness, in relation to the particular histories, circumstances, and purposes that intersect in a given life. Because illness is so concrete and so intensely personal, it resists generalizations and offers, instead, a great multiplicity of truths. We need only listen for these truths to emerge, and a good friend helps us to do that listening by setting aside preconceived notions and patiently bearing witness. This listening, the careful attending to the particulars of one's own experience (that muddle of odd sensations, startling dreams, and bizarre associations), is the great labor of illness. It is a delicate process that can easily be disturbed by the wrong sort of advice—and enhanced by the thoughtful reflection of another. One of the most valuable gifts I received during my illness was a painting a friend made of a dream I had, and told him, about being sick. I hung it over the door to my bedroom, so that I could see it when I was lying in bed, and that painting, with its image of fingers of sunlight reaching into the dark folds of a lush landscape, has nourished me ever since, because it reflects my dream back to me magnified through the eyes and heart of my friend.

Whether we come to realize our illnesses are accidents of birth, the result of radiation exposure, God's punishment, or God's grace, there is always a teaching to be found. That does not necessarily mean that teaching is the purpose of illness, or that sick people are more in need of that advice; it is just an inevitable outcome of the profound transformations that come with the territory. In the terrible clarity of the nearness of death, what Hobbie termed "ignorance," as it exists in ourselves and our world, is stripped away, if only for a moment. Our lives condense, collapse, and recoalesce, requiring changes, and we are responsible to those changes. We are not responsible *for* our illnesses, we are responsible *to* them,[10] to what they offer and require of all of us, sick and well alike.

THE EXORCISM OF DECAY

About a year after I was diagnosed with CFIDS, I dreamed that I went to the doctor for tests. After taking a sample of my saliva, she returned to say they could not run the tests because they found the semen of the man who molested me as a child in my saliva. She told me I would have to keep returning for tests until the semen was gone, so I could sign the Declaration of Independence(!). At the time I knew the dream was referring to the legacy of my early abuse experiences; I had recently finished a few years of therapy dealing with it. What I did not fully realize then was that my illness would help my body eject that poison.

In the months that followed that dream I had several episodes of sudden nausea, shaking, and vomiting that threw me back into the memory of those childhood ordeals. I simply became that panic-stricken one-year-old gagging on semen; sometimes it felt as though there was a tornado inside of my body shredding my insides. These flashbacks were terrifying and exhausting; they rank among the most difficult experiences I have ever endured. But once they passed, I often felt extraordinarily calm and strangely radiant, as if bathed in light, as only newborns can be.

I remember one of those episodes in particular, because I went through it alone for the first time, terrified I would shatter like glass and fly apart into a million pieces, never to come back together. At one point I caught a glimpse of myself in the bathroom mirror as I stood up from vomiting and felt such a sudden rush of compassion for the child I saw there that my breath returned and I calmed down. When I lay back down, I had a flash of seeing how the scheme of my life and all my experiences fit together as a congruent whole—a vision that sustains me to this day.

A few minutes later a friend stopped by and found me trembling on the couch, my face wet with tears. She knelt on the floor and held me in her arms, silently. I knew she felt deep sorrow for me, but I did not have the means to tell her of that luminous vision; I could not even reassure her that I was all right. The sacred transmutations that occur in the nether regions of illness, in the mute matter of our bodies, are often too primordial and otherworldly to articulate, communicate, or even remember, but they still hold effect.

Illness is such a good means for eliminating toxins, the ingrained poisons in our physical, mental, and emotional anguish. It pushes us, through unending frustrations, beyond the point of caring and clutching. Whatever waits in the wings of our psyches—the buried memory, unshed tears, hidden yearning, or radiant vision—is flushed to the surface. The small failures, indignities, and dependencies of illness (having to miss a work deadline, smell bad to a new lover, or ask a favor of a neighbor) open pockets of self-loathing that we usually manage to avoid. We are repeatedly asked to accept, and even find mercy for, those parts of ourselves we find most distasteful: the nag, crybaby, martyr, or addict. Illness, like so many forms of adversity, brings out the worst in us while requiring the most of us, and it works this exorcism of sorts through the very features we find so offensive in the sick: the bad breath, runny noses, and oozing sores, the coughing, spitting, crying, and vomiting.

These are the sights and smells of a body, mere matter, in the process of decay. I remember looking at my lover's father when he was dying of cancer, laid out like tracks in a hospital bed, his thin translucent skin melting into the contours of bone. I thought to myself: He could be a pile of leaves on a forest floor some warm, rainy April day, succumbing to the ancient and inevitable rites of decomposition.

No wonder we speak of breaking down or falling apart when we are sick; we are literally and figuratively decomposing. Not surprisingly, images of decay and fragmentation frequent the writings of sick people. Laura Chester compared herself to a "bust-up pile of kindling, left in preparation for some big bonfire," when she was bedridden with lupus.[11] After a year of illness I found myself staring one day at an illustration in a science book of the "agents of decay"—termites, centipedes, ticks, mites, earthworms, fungi, bacteria, parasites, and more—with a newfound fascination, realizing that many were at work, right then, in the warm tropics of my body. Sometimes, when I could not sleep at night, I entertained myself by imagining sordid scenes of decay: bugs crawling and gnawing in the woodwork behind wallpaper, food rotting, swelling, and growing fuzz in the dumpsters behind restaurants.

Illness, like death, is a dirty, messy vegetative process. In a fever my insides feel like soup on the stove, or compost in the bin, percolating. I rumble, shiver and sweat, burp and fart, and drink vast quantities of liquid—all of which work to soften the rigid, eliminate the unnecessary, and reduce wholes to their original parts. Illness effects its cure, as Hippocrates first pointed out, through a natural process of "coction" or boiling, that disintegrates old forms and coalesces new ones; one of the Navajo words for disease actually translates as "fragmentation and reassemblage." This is the sacred alchemy we witness every fall, in the dropping of sap, the moldering of leaves, and the scattering of seed, reminding us that life requires death, just as activity needs rest, and health feeds on illness, in the ongoing cycle of creation. The powers of decay, which operate with the ruthless detachment of all scavengers, do not care whether we are fat or skinny, good or bad, eating low-fat yogurt or steaks every night; they just do the work that is required—transformation—to restore equilibrium to an imbalanced system. Disease and death are not failures of life; they are part of the cycle of life, in fact, the very means of its continuation.

THE STRUGGLE TO BE

The metabolic processes of self-healing—breakdown and rebuilding—continually occur in our bodies without our ever knowing. Food is digested, hair grows, and paper cuts disappear in a matter of days, as our bodies—and souls—constantly ingest and adapt to our environments, maintaining an ever-fluctuating homeostasis. Our skin is replaced every month, the skeleton every three months, and the stomach lining every four days, while our psyches spin dreams to repair the tapestry of our lives every night. These are the daily, indeed hourly, miracles we rarely notice, which prompt many healers of all persuasions (including some doctors) to assert that our bodies heal themselves by way of nature, and only occasionally find use for outside assistance. Disease is the externalization of that ongoing healing, giving us the rare opportunity to witness a process that is usually invisible and unconscious.

The healing that also manifests as disease is a very natural process, but it does not occur without struggle, for life is dynamic, constantly fluctuating between states of order and chaos. "Like every factor of disequilibrium," observed E. M. Cioran, "sickness arouses—whips up and encourages an element of tension and conflict."[12] While this conflict reflects the loss of equilibrium, it also provides the means for its recovery in a creative resolution of tensions, a more complex order of being, in the uncanny wisdom of evolution.

There are struggles with physical limitation in illness, the pain, weakness, and fatigue that so quickly erode our pride and aspirations and make simple tasks, even breathing, so difficult. But the pressures of these limitations call forth a deeper struggle which is ongoing within us but usually unconscious—that of the self in its efforts to be, to unfold and fulfill its purpose. Inevitably, at some point in the course of a lengthy illness—for me it happened when

I was standing in front of the refrigerator one day—the startling question arises: Who am I?

Contradictions of character—tenderness and cruelty, faith and despair—emerge and collide under the pressures of illness, necessitating some kind of reformulation. Denton Welch wrote that during the long bedridden days of his recovery, the faces of people he had known flashed before his eyes as the very "embodiments of my good and bad qualities come to visit and haunt me."[13] No wonder sick people often appear to be split personalities; we flip between extremes—hot and cold, drowsy and alert, stingy and forgiving, cheerful and despondent—in a matter of moments. These oscillations make us keenly aware of the opposites that reside within us; many sick people speak of learning to "walk a tightrope" between these extremes, or of searching for the "eye of the cyclone," which is the work of reconciliation.

In the breakdown of illness, the many parts of ourselves, realized and unrealized, swirl about in a turbulent confusion; it is not uncommon for an old established construct of character to give way, while hidden, neglected parts of ourselves surface in sudden reversals of mood, thought, or behavior. I have a friend who is ordinarily quite comfortable living with a mess, but when she gets sick, she cleans it all up, throwing out old newspapers, scrubbing the counters, and folding her clothes in a fevered frenzy. Occasionally whole new personalities emerge under the influence of illness; I have known extroverts to become hermits, and shy lovers to turn lascivious. These sudden transformations can be disconcerting, if not frightening, to those who love, need, or care for someone who is sick; my lover gave names to a couple of the strange characters who emerged in me during my illness—a belligerent two-year-old, a secretive poet—and often asked me, "Who are you now?"

As the buried potentials within ourselves begin to emerge, the conscious attachments and identifications that had kept them underfoot for so long are thrown into sharp relief. Sick people often speak of having to drop the masks and roles they have assumed for the sake of others; in fact, many feel that their lives—and souls—depend upon it. Oliver Sacks wrote that he had to relinquish the "active, masculine, ordering self, which I had equated with my science, my self-respect, my mind," in order to heal.[14] Many women, like myself, wrestle with a tyrannical perfectionism that insists that every task be completed—every dish washed and letter answered—before sitting down to rest, or write, or do whatever it is that gives us pleasure.

These are the parts of ourselves that assume control and impose expectations that distort and deny our true selves; at some point they become dangerous to our health. The neglected parts of ourselves can actually become toxic, as a rotting body would, if not allowed some expression. According to Iroquois cosmology (as reported by seventeenth-century Jesuit missionaries), some diseases result from the resentment of a soul whose desires are not being met.[15] These desires of the soul are not the same as our usual conscious desires; they dwell deep within our hearts and reveal themselves only through dreams, which speak their language. When those desires are denied—which is easy to do in a culture like ours which ignores dreams—the Iroquois say the soul revolts against the body, causing diseases and even death. That is why so many sick people insist that they will die if they do not . . . get back to painting or have a child or leave their marriage, and why Audre Lorde offered the following secret of healing: "Find some particular thing your soul craves for nourishment and do it."[16]

In shamanic traditions, soul loss is one of the major and most serious causes of illness. It often occurs when a person suffers severe trauma, such as an accident, assault, or death of a loved one, and loses some of his or her vital essence.[17] Some people describe it as feeling a hole in their souls. A part of ourselves separates, and often gets lost or forgotten; if it does not return, we shuffle through life without full memory of our histories, feeling alienated and dissociated, weak and vulnerable to spiritual intrusions: the malice of others and viral attack. Illness, and even death, commonly result.

"It is becoming increasingly clear," wrote Jeanne Achterberg, professor of psychology and physical medicine, "that what the shamans refer to as soul loss—that is, injury to the inviolate core which is the essence of a person's being—does manifest as despair, immunological damage, cancer, and a host of other very serious disorders."[18]

The process of soul retrieval, as practiced by shamans of many traditions, is a very difficult, dangerous, and technically sophisticated art, of which I have limited knowledge. However, it seems clear to me that one of the tasks of illness, and requirements of healing, is to reclaim one's soul—that vital essence that enables us to thrive—and resume one's "path of destiny." We can do that informally by calling up our lost memories and reinhabiting them (which the sleepless nights and forced inactivity of illness facilitate), by listening to our dreams and intuitions, and by being honest with ourselves and others about our true feelings and desires, which the extremities of illness and the threat of death make so painfully evident. Only by facing the unvarnished facts of oneself—one's unhappiness in a marriage, for example, or need to return to the piano—can we arrive at the solutions that comprise healing; no amount of positive thinking, when forced rather than felt, can make them appear.

We also nourish our souls by doing those things that make us feel happy, fulfilled, or right with ourselves and the world for even one moment, no matter how sick we are. Writing has been my soul-saving activity since I have been sick; no matter how bad I felt or how poorly my mind worked, a few hours of writing left me feeling better about myself and more reconciled with my circumstances. I have wanted to write for years, but always found reasons not to; there were bills to pay, children to raise, careers to establish, political injustices to protest . . . but beneath all these imperatives was the notion that I had nothing important to say, and the conviction that I did not deserve to be happy while others were not. It has taken this illness, a few years of therapy, and the authority of midlife to erode that thinking and allow myself to write—and thrive.

Evidently, the forces of decay and destruction that operate in illness facilitate subtle, though critical, reformulations of self that give our souls a little more room to breathe. Once tensions build to a critical mass and the old order finally gives way, one is often struck by an extraordinary sense of peace, the sensation of a newfound equilibrium. Laura Chester described it well: After months of aching, tossing and turning in her bed, wrestling with the questions of a lifetime, she "felt something give, as if an old rotten rope had finally lost its grip on the pier's post, and I was released into a greater lake, a wider gentleness."[19] Afterward she wondered why she had struggled for so long against that kindness, rejecting peace for direction.

This is how illness can function to compensate for one-sidedness, reestablish equilibrium, and allow new solutions to evolve, on a metabolic level as well as the psychological; one could say it is a call for self-realization, whether it ends in death or recovery. This is the way of nature, the wisdom of vegetative processes. While these processes are always operating within us, in illness, injury, or death they are quickened, intensified, and externalized, eliciting our conscious participation in the ongoing work of transformation.

Because we are dealing with vegetative processes, it is appropriate that we call upon the ancient, redemptive consciousness of plants to address the crises of illness. After all, most of our medicines come from plants, and many shamans receive their visions for healing with the aid of an ingested plant. Since I have been sick, plants have populated my dreams with uncanny frequency; only recently, as my health has improved, have I begun to dream of animals. There have been cornstalks and morning glories, turning maples and blooming poppies, fields of ripe wheat rippling in the wind, prickly pear cacti waiting for rain to bloom, and the dark tangled roots of an herb. They have carried me through the worst of my illness by speaking of rising and falling and rising again, waiting with the stillness of hidden roots, bending with the weight of forces beyond my control, winding my way around adversity and then using it for support. These are wisdoms I need now to counter the willful assumptions and impositions, toxic attitudes and behaviors, that became my habit in the ease and excess of health.

5

THE ALCHEMY OF ILLNESS

The greatest treasure comes out of the most despised and secret places. . . . This place of greatest vulnerability is also a holy place, a place of healing. . . .

—Albert Kreinheder[1]

Curiously, the work of decay is facilitated by hordes of the very same microscopic organisms—fungi, bacteria, and parasites—we blame for many diseases. They break down the order of systems into a disarray of parts, translating dead matter into essential nutrients, to feed the next generation, and our warm, moist anaerobic insides provide the perfect environment for their invisible labors. Physicists write formulas for the magical transmutations of matter and energy, but the ancient goddesses and gods of creation have stirred their sticks in this bubbling cauldron of life, the dark fomenting waters of chaos, from the beginning of time.

After I had been sick for several months, it became clear to me that I was changing in fundamental ways and that I would never go back to my "old self." One day, when I was taking my morning walk across the mesa, I heard myself muttering under my breath, over and over like a droning chant, "I don't know who I am anymore.

I don't know who I am anymore." Like many sick people, I had begun to realize that my illness was not so much a state of being as a process of transformation. My body was changing, losing weight, luster, and vitality, while assuming an ethereal tenor, just as my interests and preferences were shifting dramatically. I yearned for some kind of map or diagram that could describe, and even predict, these strange mutations of character I felt myself undergoing.

Then one day, as I stood in my kitchen stirring powdered vitamin C into a glass of water, staring at the vast array of medicinal bottles on the counter, I realized that my illness and its healing were matters of chemistry. That chemistry was very physical, as in the magnesium and potassium I took to help my body assimilate the vitamin C, but there was something more to it, for there were times when remedies worked, or did not work, for no apparent reason. For example, I often felt better as soon as I swallowed my vitamin C, long before it had time to take effect. Medical researchers call it the "placebo effect"; I prefer to call it magic, for it occurs when something—a pill or a word—is imbued with power and meaning, and so becomes more effective. That is alchemy.

DECAY AND THE BEGINNING OF THE GREAT WORK

Like many schooled in the scientific worldview, I once had the impression that the alchemists of medieval and Renaissance Europe were misguided fools at best, greedy charlatans at worst, who tried to turn lead into gold in their secret laboratories. While some may have been just that, many were astute observers of the transformations that occur in visible and invisible realms; their experiments form the basis of modern chemistry and homeopathy, while informing the practice of modern psychotherapy and astrology. Carl Jung was among the first in this century to revive their teachings; he and his followers interpreted their arcane formulas metaphorically, which was the mode of thought at that time, and so made their enormous insights available to us.[2] Under Jung's keen perception, alchemy emerged as an eloquent model of the stages and processes of spiritual evolution—one which has offered me much-needed comfort and guidance in coping with the vicissitudes of illness.

One of the central tenets of alchemical philosophy was that physical decay is the beginning of the "Great Work": spiritual transformation. Paracelsus, a renowned physician and alchemist of the sixteenth century, wrote: "Decay is the beginning of all birth . . . the midwife of very great things!", adding that this is "the deepest mystery and miracle that He [God] has revealed to mortal man."[3] People who have endured great physical trauma—car accidents, war injuries, surgery, or torture—occasionally bear witness to this mystery with stories of tunnels of light, angelic presences, and religious conversions. In one of my memories of being molested as a baby, it seemed as though my body tore open and I flew through space into the lap of two enormously comforting presences; throughout my childhood, I referred to them as my "pink parents in the sky." Physical pain cancels the claims of the world and the hold of ordinary consciousness, opening us to the unworldly forces of the metaphysical. No wonder the image of Jesus suffering on the cross is the central symbol of spiritual rebirth in Christianity.

Alchemists began the Great Work of spiritual transformation with what they called *prima materia,* the basic matter or problem. In their efforts to make gold, they did not start with refined or precious metals, such as silver or copper, but with the most common, base, and ugly of metals: lead. In psychological terms, this means the work of spiritual transformation springs from the places we feel most inferior or debased. Alchemists outlined four qualities that can help us to find and identify this ever-so-promising matter: (1) It is ordinary and found everywhere; (2) people are often revolted by it; (3) it has many names and faces but only one essence; (4) it is boundless, consuming, and overwhelming. In summary, *prima materia* is that which is everywhere, unavoidable, despicable, and out of control in our lives: the diseases of our bodies and souls. Is it any wonder that many Renaissance physicians were also alchemists?

Alchemists put this bothersome matter into a closed container and cooked it; it is important to note that they did not add or subtract anything, but simply dissolved the matter in its own water. In so doing, they amplified the distress until the matter transformed of its own accord, in the recognition that healing is derived from the illness itself. Paracelsus explained that each disease "bears its own remedy within itself. . . . Health must grow from the same root as disease."[4] This understanding forms the basis for the homeopathic practice of treating like with like and the psychotherapeutic practice of active listening, in which counselors repeat and rephrase the key themes of their clients' stories until the clients themselves arrive at some conclusion. It is also echoed in the words of many sick people who discover, after searching in vain for a cure, that the answers cannot be found outside oneself; they must come from within.

Jungian analyst Arnold Mindell, who works with sick and dying people, has taken the alchemical practice of "cooking the matter" one step further, by encouraging his clients to exaggerate their symptoms until they reach some kind of breakthrough: relief or realization. Mindell developed his approach after observing that people often unconsciously respond to physical discomfort by doing something to make it worse; for example, someone with eczema or poison ivy is apt to scratch it until it is fully inflamed, while people with stiff necks often bend their heads backwards to feel the pain. One day, when Mindell was watching his son pick a scab on his knee, making it bleed, he realized that our bodies actually try to make pain worse.[5]

I know that urge to pick a scab, scratch a mosquito bite, or press on a bruise; it is almost irresistible and strangely hypnotic, like many body impulses, including sexual ones. Since I have been sick with CFIDS, I have noticed in myself a tendency to push some of my symptoms, such as depression, fatigue, and mental confusion, to their breaking point. When my mood droops, I inevitably start to catalogue everything wrong with myself and the world until I am violently depressed and crying into my pillow. When my memory begins to fail, I call one wrong number after another hoping to remember the right one, or drive down street after street looking for a friend's house, until I finally give in and give up. That is what I call my "boiling point," and I usually dissolve into tears, fall asleep for a few minutes, and wake resolved to rest more often. These symptoms actually necessitate what the doctor who first diagnosed me termed "the only remedy" for CFIDS: rest. In extremity, symptoms reveal their own remedies.

The alchemists insisted that two things must happen before the cure can be extracted from the disease: The problem must be kept in a closed container, and it must be reduced to its original state through a process of breakdown. The limitations and immobility of illness provide the closed container that enables this transformation, precisely because there is no way out. Early on in my illness my dreams offered the image of a snarl of snakes stuck in a bottle for my situation; alchemical texts are filled with images of dangerous animals—lions or wolves—trapped in the chemist's flask. Alice James called herself "bottled lightning . . . a geyser of emotions, sensations, speculations, and reflections fermenting . . . in my poor old carcass" when she was dying of cancer.[6] The isolation and lack of sympathy or understanding that sick people often endure may even be necessary to secure the walls of the container, so that nothing is spilled or shared and the matter inside will reach the point of transmutation. The walled space of illness, like therapy, intensifies the brooding and incubates the egg.

Most religious traditions actually prescribe the disciplines that illnesses impose—abstinence, isolation, and stillness—creating artificial walled spaces for the purposes of spiritual development. The Asclepian temples of ancient Greece contained private incubation chambers where sick people would lie down, drift into an altered state of twilight sleep, and receive the ministrations of the healing gods and goddesses; could it be that we are more amenable to their touch in a place of stillness and isolation? Whether confined by the small circle of a sweat lodge, the four walls of a monk's cell, or the four posts of the sickbed, the mind cannot be distracted by the tasks of movement, and so turns back upon itself, in the downward, inward spiral of a whirlpool. While at first I often feel trapped, and sometimes panic for fear of losing my mind, I inevitably come to cherish the immense sense of leisure and inner spaciousness I discover when freed from drive and desire.

Occasionally, and most often unexpectedly, the mind loses itself momentarily, and profound shifts of perception occur that are the stuff of healing and enlightenment. Arnold Beisser described one such experience: One evening, not long after he was paralyzed by polio, Beisser was lying alone, feeling particularly helpless and bored, staring down an empty corridor, wishing someone or something would appear. No one came, and his depression grew into despair until he felt as though he could no longer stand it. Then, he wrote, "I began to see variations, shades of gray and darkness, shadows and light. The doorways opening onto the corridor formed subtle geometric patterns according to the different ways the doors were ajar. I began to look carefully and wonder at this scene that only a few moments before had depressed me so. It now seemed startlingly beautiful. . . . I do not know how the perception arrived or why it left, but from then on I understood that what I sought was possible. My task was to discover how to change from one state to another."[7]

Much as sick people complain, often vociferously, about their isolation and the lack of sympathy from others (we constantly switch doctors and friends in search of the "good ear"), many come to recognize that this invisible wall between the sick and the well protects both. Laura Chester wrote that "the isolation of illness did not seem to be a bad thing," for she was "left alone to revive the inner seed, which had withered under the intensity of interaction."[8] There came a point in the depths of my illness when I realized that the people closest to me could no longer bear to hear of my despair, which was inconsolable; it seemed to short-circuit their capacities for attention and compassion. After a long night of self-confrontation, I decided to keep that bitter nest of despair to myself from then on—and a curious shift occurred. While I felt scared, like a lost child whose cries could not be heard, I also felt infused with power, a power I associate with mountain climbers and deep-sea divers, people who face their destiny and know their survival rests in their own two hands. I felt, to use Chester's words, "my soul opening and strengthening, like a muscle."

Not only is it better for the sick to be left alone at times; it is also better for the well to leave them at times. Healthy people can be contaminated by the gloom and depression of the ailing if they come too close or have too much sympathy; it is commonly called burnout in the helping professions. If that were to happen too often, as Virginia Woolf surmised, "buildings would cease to rise; roads would peter out into grassy tracks; there would be an end of music and of paintings"[9]; for culture is created and maintained by those with the energy, enthusiasm, and idealism of health. The well need to be well for the world to continue, just as the sick need to be sick so the world can be regenerated. Each has a necessary job to perform.

THE OPERATIONS OF BREAKDOWN

In the closed container of the alchemist's flask, the problem is reduced, broken down, and returned to its original state of disorder, which the alchemists termed *massa confusa*, meaning confused mass. One of my dreams offered a wonderful description of this breakdown: A young woman had a neurological disorder that scrambled the words of her statements, turning them into questions—in French, no less. What has been learned under the assumptions of health must be unlearned under the exigencies of disease. Sick people often speak of peeling back the layers of a lifetime like an onion, for the deepest parts of ourselves are also the oldest. Homeopathists and acupuncturists point out that in healing we work back through every illness we have had, in reverse order, until we eventually arrive at the root, which may be variously described as a genetic inclination, a predilection of character, one's karma or destiny. These origins are almost too profound and ethereal to identify, except in the altered states of illness. As Mary Winfrey Trautmann observed of her daughter when she was sick with leukemia, "I sense a transformation occurring, even as I watch, a change I cannot analyze—except to note that she seems to be growing younger. She is a child, sleeping, moving away from me, through dreams involved with mysterious transactions in which I have no part."[10]

Alchemists identified many processes that facilitate this breakdown, loss of composure, and return to origins. Four of the most basic ones—*calcinatio* (burning by fire), *solutio* (dissolving in water), *sublimatio* (rising in air), and *coagulatio* (falling into earth)—were associated with the elements of fire, water, air, and earth, which are so evident in illness. While these processes were often described as stages, they do not occur in any particular sequence; we slip in and out of them, back and forth among them, spending more time in some than others, according to our temperamental inclinations, and the requirements of our souls.

Calcinatio is a burning process most evident in fevers, but it is also associated with the intensity of frustrated desires. How many times have we heard ourselves say, "I'm burning up inside," or "she's burning" with anger, resentment, or envy? There is no doubt about it, we cannot get much of what we want—sleep, pleasure, activity, or company—when we are sick, and we rarely manage to accommodate ourselves to these losses. We are impossibly frustrated every night we cannot sleep, angry every time we cannot go out, envious when our friends go off skiing, resentful when they eat the foods forbidden us. This struggle is the burning of *calcinatio*, and one is quickly reminded that passions are their own punishment, as the Buddhists claim.

Alchemical texts assert that the process of *calcinatio* produces salt, which manifests as bitterness, until it is further purified into wisdom. This observation makes me wonder whether the interventions of modern medicine lock us into bitterness and keep us from the promise of wisdom by intercepting the disease process, which is also, in alchemical terms, the process of enlightenment. Illnesses have their own timing; as John Donne observed, "a sickness must ripen of itself, [we] cannot hasten it."[11]

Solutio is a dissolving process that melts walls and rigidities, opening us up to the full chaos and mystery of life, often with a great surge of emotion. This process usually starts with a sense of confusion or disorientation; sick people often wander into strange rooms at all hours of day and night, only to stop with startled looks, as if to ask, "What am I doing here?" Standing with furrowed brows, we may hear the clock ticking, see the shadows cast by a streetlight, and feel a dampness in the air, but not know what any of it means. Emotions catch in our throats and tears are common under the sway of *solutio*, tears of frustration or unexpected relief, sorrow, or joy. There are moments of great fear, when shadows assume demonic shapes, but there are also times of euphoria, when the tinkles of chandeliers become the voices of angels. Robert Murphy described the euphoria that followed his back operation in this way: "I seemed able to reach out and touch, almost embrace and engulf, everybody around me. I loved people, all people! . . . It is difficult to recall those feelings now, but it seemed that the sharp edges of myself had become porous and weak. People could reach into me more easily, and they, in turn, were more vulnerable to me. . . . I was suffused with a kind of peacefulness, almost a sense of joy."[12]

In the process of *sublimatio* we rise, like smoke from a fire, above ourselves to assume a more remote, encompassing vision; some would call it dissociation or leaving one's body. I imagine that my memories of watching myself being molested as a child from the ceiling were very literal instances of *sublimatio*, as are the times when I can understand, dispassionately, that it was somehow necessary for my abuser and me to go through that horror. *Sublimatio* is a transcendence, a journey to higher realms, and it offers extraordinary revelations. Carl Jung described floating high in space after his heart attack, watching "the globe of the earth, bathed in a gloriously blue light." Moments like these help us to disidentify from our bruised and burning bodies, enabling us to escape the suffering temporarily; the visions they inspire ultimately help us to endure and redeem that suffering.

The last alchemical operation, *coagulatio*, is quite evident in illness. It relates to the element of earth and represents the ways in which we are confined or bound by physical existence, by the necessities of our bodies and souls. Under the pressure and coercion of disease, we lose the spaciousness, freedom, and ease we had come to assume in health; here we encounter the fierce limits of our destinies, limits we have not chosen but must endure and be shaped by. A painter friend of mine who has developed rheumatoid arthritis in recent years can work only on her good days because her fingers are so swollen and gnarled with pain. She used to paint huge sweeping canvases; now she paints miniatures.

The mythic images of bondage, servitude, and captivity describe this suffering of one's fate, one's lot in life. Rarely do we resign ourselves peaceably, in sickness or in health; we are always hoping, always seeking the remedy that will work, only to meet with one disappointment after another, each more bitter than the last.

Eventually we surrender, realizing there is no way out but through, and start to cultivate the fine art of accommodation—learning how to live well, and gracefully, within our limitations. My friend with arthritis has provided me with a shining example; she frequently requests assistance from others, but never resorts to begging, demanding, or apologizing, because she conserves her energy and carefully defines what she is able to do each day. When we acknowledge our limitations, things come together, condensing and coalescing into a more visible form; there is fear, the sense of defeat and resignation, but also self-recognition, a strengthened resolve, and a newfound dignity. Robert Murphy wrote that after living a few years in a wheelchair, considering suicide and deciding against it, he realized that he would just have to "make the best of it with my remaining capabilities. It then occurred to me that this is the universal human condition. We all have to muddle through life within our limitations. . . ."[13] This is the heroism of daily living, in which we learn to abide by the requirements and limitations of our circumstances through the long custom of surrender.

All four processes of breakdown—*calcinatio, solutio, sublimatio,* and *coagulatio*—end in "*mortificatio,*" meaning decay or death-making, one of the most important stages of the alchemical process; in fact, it is the bottom, the critical turning point of the entire labor. *Mortificatio,* which is also known as the "*nigredo,*" or blackening, is the experience of defeat, failure, and humiliation, which the disabilities and dependencies of illness certainly inspire. The process was often pictured in alchemical texts as an old king, or a young innocent, laid out on his deathbed, images that have popped up regularly in my dreams since I developed CFIDS. To the extent that we derive our self-worth from our abilities, our aspirations, or the appearances we maintain, we are "mortified" by their loss in the devastations of illness. We feel beaten, ground down, and crushed by the unending series of small failures—the missed deadlines, spilled food, and unkind remarks. One of the most difficult things I have had to deal with in my illness is the fact that I could no longer reliably do the quality of work I had come to expect of myself. I cringed every time I had to send out an article with run-on sentences, or apologize to a client for forgetting something. *Mortificatio* whittles us down to size—and a very small one at that.

I suspect that one must become very small in order to pass through the valley of illness; in that smallness we are made painfully aware of our faults and failings. We hover over recent embarrassments and shameful memories, beat and work over what is the matter with us in the confines of our own rooms during those long afternoons and nights when we cannot sleep. *Coagulatio* and *mortificatio* are by nature guilt-ridden processes. Standing in the shadows of our former selves, we are made to taste the stuff of our own dirt.

THE PHILOSOPHER'S STONE

There came a point in my illness, just as I was starting to get a little more energy back, when I fell into a state of intense despair and could not get out of it, much to my fright and shame. I hated life so vehemently I could not sleep, taste food, or enjoy sex; I envied my healthy, happy friends so much that I started making cruel remarks to cut them down to size. I was horrified to see how quickly and easily my usual faith and compassion gave way, and in circumstances much less trying than many endure. At first I blamed it on my illness, which is known to cause neurological disturbances, but eventually I realized that it was *my* depression, even if it was triggered by CFIDS, that I had seen it before and would probably see it again, and it was up to me to figure out how to come to terms with it. I felt small, dirty, and tainted by my own faultiness (like "a can of worms" as I told my lover), but on the other hand, something in me thrilled to the challenge of cracking this nut, of chewing the gristle, simply because it was mine to crack or chew. I decided to stop complaining and just sit with my dirt.

My dreams became unusually lucid, like open palms divulging their secrets, giving me clear advice. They told me that hatred is not to be avoided or indulged, but offered back to the powers of the deep, for their own inscrutable purposes; that faith is not something you must have or cannot lose, but something you practice because the world depends on it. I started making daily prayers, and though I fumbled with inexperience, they helped. One of my dreams encouraged me to make a place for my pack of black dogs—my despair, envy, and hate—at the end of my bed.

Perhaps there was also a dog by the name of greed, for in another dream I could not get gas for my car until I admitted my greed. That was difficult, for greed is a quality I detest in others, but eventually I found the part of myself that wants it all for myself, the part of me that secretly hoards ice cream, books, and money. Then my dream took an interesting turn: When the gas station attendant put gas in my car, I realized that I needed my greed, in the form of strong, selfish desires, in order to get going! So when my doctor offered me a remedy for serotonin (one of the neurotransmitters that affects mood, which is commonly disturbed by CFIDS), I took it greedily, and within a few days the shell of my despair cracked. It is not that I never feel despair or envy or hatred—I still do at times, but the feelings pass and I do not get stuck in them anymore. In the metaphor of my dream, they sleep at the end of my bed.

To this day, I do not know whether it was the serotonin remedy that dispelled my despair or the fact that I had to eat my shadow and claim my greed in order to take it; perhaps these seemingly separate events were simultaneous reflections in the mirrors of my body and soul. Herein lies one of the keynotes of alchemical philosophy: that all things are related to their opposites, and the goal, whether it be known as spiritual revelation, self-realization, or healing, always involves the reunion of opposites. Magic is present in those sacred spaces where opposites touch—at dawn and dusk when day meets night, at the edges of sleep where dreaming and waking realities mingle, and wherever ego touches archetype in the midst of defeat or the postures of prayer. Miracles of healing can occur at these intersections, although they are not necessary or inevitable, but simply demonstrations of grace.

For someone like me, who tends toward excessive sympathy and strident idealism, a good dose of greed, hatred, and despair are just what the doctor ordered. Actually, it would be more accurate to say that as my character boiled in the closed container of my illness, my darker sides emerged as warnings and as needed antidotes. When my despair emerged to counter my idealism and my resentments met my compassion, a tremendous energy for healing was released; I think of it as the spirit in the bottle, the homeopathic remedy.

Now that I am—hopefully—through the worst of it, I feel very lucky and eternally grateful for the hands that helped me through those straits to reclaim some lost parts of myself. I cannot forget that those places and my capacity to choose them exist within me, nor can I forget what I have learned about my own fragility and that of the world, so the prayers continue. At the same time, I feel more solid, as though finally standing on both my feet for the first time in my life, as if the pale outline of myself had at last been filled in with color. This combination of fragility and strength is just one of the many curious contradictions that come true in the midst of illness. As the alchemists often said, the "sun and its shadow" complete the work.

As we accept the shadow, we are naturally humbled. Hubris, which translates as going "beyond the allotted portion," our so-human desire to push our limits and feel powerful, is slain in illness, to nurture reverence and humility, the simple recognition of our human littleness in relation to a greater Mystery. Disease, defeat, and the humility they inspire actually constellate the numinous powers of nature and the soul, just as the vast expanses of sea, sky, or canyon cliffs call forth our awe.

In alchemical terms, base matter is transmuted through the process of death into gold, the philosopher's stone, the self-realization that heals all by combining opposites and rectifying one-sidedness. Illness operates upon the stuff of our bodies to reveal and release that spiritual essence—our unique natures, powers, and virtues—which lie buried in the body "like a mummy in a tomb," to quote Paracelsus. It is a process of development that just carries "to its end something that has not yet been completed," as the alchemists often insisted.

Not long ago, when I turned down an invitation to attend a Buddhist meditation retreat because I was not well enough to sit upright for hours, I felt sad, wondering when I would be able to resume spiritual practices. Then, as I was falling asleep that night, it occurred to me that my illness is my spiritual path and practice—at least for now.

6

THE UNDERWORLD JOURNEY

This limbo—which lasted for twelve timeless days—started as torment, but turned into patience; started as hell, but became a purgatorial dark night; humbled me, horribly, took away hope, but then sweetly-gently, returned it to me thousandfold, transformed.

—Oliver Sacks[1]

After three years of illness I had a dream in which I came upon a grievous sight: the body of a lion sprawled across the ground in the savannas of Africa, apparently dying. The lion had been shot with a poison arrow by an English colonialist, and none of the native people gathered around knew what kind of poison it was, so they could not treat the great beast. "If only the lion could talk," someone said. I promptly decided to swallow the poison myself—even though it could kill me—in order to describe my symptoms so the people could find the proper antidote. I remember lying next to the great bulk of the lion, barely conscious, and mumbling things to the natives who bent over to listen. Then the scene shifted, and a friend gave me a beautiful jacket; as I put it over my shoulders, I saw that it was made from the mane of a lion. When I woke from that dream, I realized that my illness had come to serve the function of initiation; it was bequeathing me a mantle of power.

In many traditional cultures people undergo initiation rites at the major turning points in life: puberty, marriage, parenthood, the assumption of vocational and social responsibilities, and death.[2] These rites are not events so much as processes, transformations triggered by contact with the sacred; they are intended to prepare the individual for the powers, privileges, and responsibilities of the phase of life they are entering, by actually cultivating the strengths and awarenesses that will be needed. Most are arranged and performed by members of the community, but occasionally initiations are spontaneously generated through severe illnesses or powerful dreams, when it seems that the spirits themselves have elected the individual. This is often the case in shamanic calling.

As a general rule, industrialized cultures lack these rites of passage. A few relics remain—baptisms, confirmations, graduations, weddings, and funerals—but they do not really try, refine, and educate the character of the individual as initiation ceremonies do. We may be handicapped by that loss more than we know; Toni Cade Bambara wrote in her novel about healing, *The Salt-Eaters,* that we must "tap the brain for any knowledge of initiation rites lying dormant there, recognizing that life depended on it, that initiation was the beginning of transformation and that the ecology of the self, the tribe, the species, the earth depended on just that."[3]

Our bodies appear to remember the formula—perhaps they generated it to begin with—and sometimes step in to meet the need. The labor of childbirth provides an initiation for both mother and child, just as the labor of dying does; illness may do the same. In fact, serious illnesses follow the stages and requirements of traditional initiation ceremonies—separation, submergence, metamorphosis, and reemergence—with remarkable fidelity, though sometimes we hover in one stage for a while, or slip back and forth between two or three of them, before emerging. I could not say that illness is equivalent to initiation, for there are depths and mysteries to those ceremonies of which I know nothing, but I have observed that some illnesses, especially those that occur in midlife, serve initiatory functions, giving us the wisdom we need to assume the lion's mantle, the authority and creative power of age.

THE PAINFUL PROCESS OF DEFOLIATION

The first stage of initiation, as identified by anthropologists, is separation from the social context. Initiates are taken, some say "stolen," from their families, sometimes without warning; the ceremonial leaders may simply show up at the door one day and lead—or drag—their charges away. Illness is equally rude in its sudden arrivals and immediate takeovers. Even though we may realize later that the signs were coming for quite some time, the element of initial shock seems to be an important ingredient in the process of initiation; it is the first step in our gradual undoing.

Initiates are taken out into the bush or the mountains, to a special sanctuary or womblike hut that is close to the potent powers of nature, while far from the influence of society. They leave behind the trappings of identity: their clothing and possessions, even their names. So too the sick leave work, retreat to the bedroom or hospital, disrobe for their doctors, sometimes forget their names, and become one of the anonymous many. Hospitals are notoriously depersonalizing, giving out numbered ID bracelets and one-size-fits-all gowns. Apparently, individuals must be removed from their immediate context and relations for initiations to proceed; the same may be true of healing with disease. Audre Lorde, who went to a clinic in Switzerland to receive treatments for cancer, explained that "sometimes we cannot heal ourselves close to the very people from whom we draw strength and light, because they are also closest to the places and tastes and smells that go along with a pattern of living we are trying to rearrange."[4]

Once removed from their families, initiates and their counterparts, the sick, enter what anthropologists have termed a "liminal" world, a sacred territory outside of ordinary time and space, beyond cultural convention, somewhere betwixt and between life and death. They are often treated like corpses or newborns, covered with blankets, ashes, or dirt and asked to lie still in little huts, caves, or hospital rooms. It is hard to tell, looking at a covered body, whether the sick person or initiate is male or female, dead or alive, rich or poor, happy or sad, as these customary distinctions dissolve into uneasy ambiguity.

Distinctions between dreaming and waking life, reality and imagination, self and other, blur; in fact, they appear to be artificial constructs. Opposites clash, reverse themselves, and sometimes merge, in dizzying patterns. Since I have been sick, there have been moments when I could not tell whether I was hot or cold, awake or dreaming, sensing something real or imagining things. I am never absolutely sure whether a particular remedy is helping or hurting me, and it seems that whenever I answer some pressing question in my life, I wake in the night in a panic of uncertainty. I start sentences and suddenly go blank in the middle, as if someone had taken an eraser and wiped away the contents of my mind with a single stroke.

Eventually we are struck dumb by the disorientations of liminality. Denton Welch described the experience well: "I found that I could not understand the meaning of anything, could explain nothing that I heard or saw. I felt myself beginning to tremble; so I said to the nurse in that steady, rather uninterested voice always kept for catastrophes, 'I don't know what anything is about. Do you?' "[5] The accumulated perceptions, assumptions, and knowledge of our life's experiences—which the Buddhists call ignorance—are shattered and scattered into useless pieces. One day, when I was complaining about not knowing what was real anymore, I remembered what a philosophy teacher of mine used to say whenever a student seemed utterly confused: "Good. Now you can begin to learn!" There is great power, "big medicine," in confusion and disorder, so much so that initiates at this stage are considered dangerous, even deadly, to the uninitiated.

Along with the confusions, there are also ordeals to be endured in the course of initiatory experiences. There are physical ordeals, those of fasting and purging, celibacy and sleeplessness, discomfort and pain, but there are also psychological ones. Initiates are often exposed in their nakedness, alternately ignored and ordered about, sometimes insulted and humiliated, and inevitably forced to face their fears in the rigor of prolonged isolation. Those who have spent any time in a hospital can attest to undergoing many, if not all, of these ordeals, and they are made all the worse by what we bring to them—our hopes and fears, attachments and resistances—the fixtures of identity and residues of a lifetime.

The anguish of illness is intensified by the confidence and pride we carry from health into the sickbed—and subsequently lose, for sickness is, among other things, a string of failures, insults, and humiliations. We fumble work, forget birthdays, yell at the children, or default on our loans, failing ourselves and others, not just once or twice, but almost every day, it seems. It is hard to be good at anything when we are sick; we cannot even keep our sheets dry or chins up all the time.

I have discovered that some of the anguish and embarrassment I have felt since being sick is self-induced; people rarely treat me badly, but I imagine how stupid, lazy, or boring I must seem to them and then feel terrible about it. At some point, in the extremity of my pain and exhaustion, I decided that I simply could not afford to judge myself so harshly; it was the proverbial straw that would break my camel's back. I have always had the tendency to be self-critical, but my illness exacerbated it to the point of self-destruction.

So I whittled my expectations down to the mean proportions of my circumstances and told myself: "The way I am right now—today—has got to be good enough," no matter how frightened, silly, stupid, or boring I am. In this move toward acceptance, this cultivated generosity of spirit, I found a modicum of peace, a tolerable way to live while sick. This is one of the ways that ordeals like illness work to destroy our bad habits, grinding us down to an open emptiness.

The word for initiation in many native languages actually means "to die." Yaya Diallo, a musician and healer from the Minianka tribe of West Africa, says that in his culture people often say, "They killed me in the initiation ceremony"; so Chekhov wrote, during his long bout with TB: "There is no more Chekhov. Illness has swallowed him." In initiation rites this death is often portrayed in gruesome detail; one is chopped or torn to pieces by monstrous spirits who then strip the flesh from the bones. When Yaya Diallo was young and about to be circumcised, the older boys told him: "The spirits will come to eat your body. Your bones will be put in the middle of a crossroads." If he was lucky, they added, he would bounce back to life. If not. . . .[6]

This imagery bears a striking resemblance to the experience of illness, for sick people often speak of being eaten up or consumed by their diseases. Since we are unable to exert much control over our bodies, thoughts, or emotional states, they run amok, scattering, like the pieces of a house swept off by a flooding river. Composure is lost. We speak of "falling apart," of being "shattered" or "undone"—the metaphors of fragmentation. In acute pain, it can feel as though knives, claws, teeth, or explosives—the tools of dismemberment—are tearing at our flesh, ripping us apart.

Many allopathic interventions actually involve some kind of dismemberment; a child with tonsillitis has his tonsils removed, and a woman with cancer may have her breast cut off. Even when we are not racked with pain or cut open by doctors, we inevitably wither away under the sway of illness; many of us lose so much weight we actually begin to look like skeletons. Carl Jung, in describing the illness that followed his heart attack at age sixty-nine, called it a "painful process of defoliation," in which "everything I aimed at or wished for or thought, the whole phantasmagoria of earthly existence, fell away or was stripped from me."[7]

A client of mine who was seriously ill for a few years with a still unidentified disease, likens her experience to the descent of Inanna, the Sumerian goddess of heaven and earth, into the underworld. Inanna had to remove every piece of her clothing and jewelry, one by one, to make it through the gates of the underworld to visit her sister; she was utterly naked by the time she arrived. Serious illness seems to take us through these same gates. When it first strikes, we leave our jobs, drop our responsibilities, stop many of our activities and pleasures, and lose our appearances; then, when illness continues, we lose our friends, our financial security, our convictions, and sometimes our marriages. Eventually illness erodes our confidence, pride, and self-respect. In the end there is only hope, and that too disappears, for when Inanna arrived in the underworld, stripped of her powers and pretenses, she was hung on a meathook to die. In the long dark night that is the fulcrum of any true experience of initiation, one cannot be assured of return; one must be still, and wait without hope.

THE TERRIBLE REVELATION

There comes a point, in the arduous journey of initiation, when one finally arrives at some primordial, mythic ground of existence; to put it another way, we develop the ability to see—if only for a few moments or hours—the invisible root essences of things and their relationships. Perhaps this is the point of the mortifications we endure, for they move us away from surface appearances into the underworld of psychic essences or shades. This is the realm of dream, myth, and imagination, a sacred space and time in which creation continually takes place, and everything, from the pattern of clouds to the color of oranges, has significance in relation to a greater whole. Black Elk, who received his great vision of the hoop of nations when he was sick, described it well: "While I stood there I saw more than I can tell and I understood more than I saw: for I was seeing in a sacred manner the shape of all shapes as they must live together like one being."[8]

While not all sick people reach this mythic underworld, remember being there, or survive to tell about it, initiates are carefully taken there and vigilantly protected from mundane influences in order to receive sacred instruction. Emptied and opened by the ordeals they have endured, they learn about the nature of things and how they came to be what they are, about the powers that generate and sustain life, and the duties we have as human beings. In the Eleusinian mysteries of ancient Greece, for example, initiates spent one night alone in the "valley of the shadow of death"; when they emerged, they were presented with a single ear of corn. That ear contained and revealed—to those finally able to see in a sacred manner—the secrets of life, death, and rebirth.

Initiates often encounter tribal ancestors and helpful and hostile spirits in the course of their journeys. Some sick people, and their close relations, have similar experiences. Recently, when I was up most of the night with nausea, the spirit of a *curandero* ministered to me just before dawn, placing a hot bowl of burning incense on my solar plexus while chanting prayers in Spanish; I was tempted to discount the experience as a figment of my sleep-deprived imagination until I realized the ceremony had worked. By the time the sun rose, the nausea was gone. A friend of mine saw Mother Mary standing on the lid of her garbage can during an allergic reaction to mold on a dark and rainy November evening; she has been building altars to Mary ever since. I have also, at times, felt the presence of threatening forces, lit candles for protection, and kept myself awake in a vigilant watch.

Mary Winfrey Trautmann confronted "Leukos," the god of white death, while her daughter Carol was dying of leukemia. When Leukos faded away, a spirit she named "the Comforter and Companion" emerged. She wrote of that mystical exchange: "Through our communication anguish and meaning both flow, the knowledge that I am part of a vast linkage to every other form, each manifestation of life, and death as well—the shapes of the blackbird as it flies, fruit ripening, the decayed stump, ashes, flesh, foam, and, my anguish speaks, to Carol's changing courses, whether they wax or wane."[9] In the extremity of her fear and grief, Trautmann received profound teachings about the nature of all things and how they are related, undergoing an initiation of her own apart from her daughter's.

Carl Jung had visions of the beginning and end of all things when he hung on the edge of death after his heart attack; he described it as an "iridescent whole" in which past, present, and future were all interwoven. Initiates are often given the opportunity to glimpse, as Jung did, the drama of ongoing creation, for to witness creation and learn how all things are put together is to be created anew, to find one's place in the cosmic order and part in sustaining that harmony. It is also to heal—whether one lives or dies, stays sick or recovers—which explains why the curing ceremonies of many native peoples involve a retelling, or reenactment, of the creation story. As the sixteenth-century physician and alchemist Gerhard Dorn observed, in order to heal, one must learn "from what one depends and to whom one belongs and to what end one has been created."[10]

THE RETURN TO RESPONSIBILITY

Contact with the mythic realm, and the knowing that that imparts, changes the very being of the initiate; he or she is never the same again. Perhaps this is why so many sick people come to divide their lives in two: before and after getting sick. Many shamans return from their initiations with an extra rib or a crystal embedded in their chests; similarly, sick people often return with scars, missing parts, pacemakers, or Jesus in their hearts. Newborn initiates are "in-formed," leaving the ignorance and irresponsibility of their youths behind, to assume the privileges and responsibilities of maturity.

The final phase of initiation—emergence from the underworld, return, and reintegration into the community—is a very delicate one, for the incessant activity of the mundane world can be painful, even devastating to the initiate so sensitized by contact with the mythic realm. Many do not make it. Since I have been getting better in recent months, I have dreamed more than once that I am a bear coming out of hibernation, all groggy and clumsy—and blinded by the light of day; in the first two dreams I just crawled right back into my hole!

Newly "hatched" initiates are often protected for a short while, sometimes rocked or suckled like newborns, to help orient them to their new lives. Similarly, people recovering from serious illnesses need a quiet place, a safe haven, where they can gradually recollect themselves and establish a new center of gravity; unfortunately, few of us get that support, as we are pushed by the demands of contemporary living back into the hustle and bustle as soon as we are able. There are debts to be paid, children to be attended to, and jobs that will not wait forever.

Many people recovering from serious illnesses or accidents report that music, rhythm, and movement help them immensely. They help us to recall ourselves into an inner harmony that gives us strength. Initiates are usually given rhythms, dances, or songs to carry with them back into the mundane world of community, and I suspect that these gifts actually ease and ensure a successful reentry by calling forth the body's memory, which is so much more detailed and accurate than words or ideas, of the mythic realities encountered during initiation. Of course, these gifts are also responsibilities; initiates are often required to perform their songs or dances at later dates, for the continued well-being of the community of life.

We too need to carry something of what we have experienced back into the world of the living, to remember the dreams, follow the imperatives, or use the powers we have been given by our sojourns in the underworld. That takes courage, clarity of mind, and the willingness to follow one's own truth even if others cannot affirm it, especially in our culture, which does not recognize the initiatory role of illness, in fact actively resists it by encouraging us to "get back to normal." If we do not carry what we have learned back into the world, we risk getting sick again, for the energies unused can revert into their destructive forms, in what I consider to be one of the hidden cruelties of illness. It has happened to many people—including Black Elk. When Black Elk first received his great vision at the ripe age of nine, he knew it was meant to be shared, but could not figure out how to do that, and so did not; eight years later he got sick again and was tormented with fears until finally an old medicine man told him that he must do what his vision wanted him to do—enact the horse dance for the people to see—and helped him do it.

When initiations are successful, the survivors slowly return to their communities with new eyes to see, new ears to hear, and the courage to act upon those perceptions. Carl Jung went on to do his most important work, explaining that "the insight that I had had, the vision of the end of all things, gave me the courage to undertake new formulations."[11] Audre Lorde spoke of feeling "another kind of power" growing within her, one that was "tempered and enduring, grounded in the realities of what I am," with the determination to "save my life by using my life in the service of what must be done."[12] Just as girls are "grown" into women through their puberty initiations, many people who have been seriously ill become what they must become, what they are meant to be, whether that occurs through death or recovery.

I like to see what people do when they recover from a serious illness; many feel an urgency to set things right. When the father of a friend of mine recovered from a heart attack, he apologized to all his children for his years of absence. Even those who are not able to recover sometimes do what they can to mend a broken world. A veteran suffering from post-traumatic stress syndrome spent two years planting trees for every American who had died in Vietnam. People with AIDS take to the streets to demand more research, improved services, and affordable drugs, even though they are not likely to live long enough to benefit from their efforts. They do so because they must, because they have been so deeply wounded—and informed—by their illnesses that they cannot do anything else. And of course there are the invisible labors that occupy so many hours of the sick and bedridden: the sorrowing for all who suffer, the remembering of those who have died, the giving of thanks for minor miracles amid major disasters, the repeated prayers and crying out for God—even the raging at God—all of which help in ways we hardly know.

And so, through processes well described by alchemical formulas and initiation rites, we are both diminished and enlarged through the agency of our illnesses, and so opened to the possibility of new life. The losses are many and visible; the harvested grain is smaller than the standing stalks, but so much more useful. So Nietzsche observed: "I doubt that such pain [the kind that compels us to descend to our ultimate depths] makes us 'better'; but I know it makes us more *profound* . . . from such abysses, from such severe sickness, one returns newborn, having shed one's skin."

7

SHAME AND THE WHITE SHADOW OF THE COLLECTIVE

We cannot afford to be without the services of rainforest, starfish or bacteria. If one part of the system becomes possessed by its "little vision"—oversteps its place in the relationship and moves in a unilateral manner—we have war or ecological crises, cancer or psychoses.

—Stephen Larsen[1]

I was intrigued to discover recently that John Donne wrote his most famous words, "No man is an island," in an essay on illness. "Every man is a piece of the Continent," he continued. "If a clod be washed away by the Sea, Europe is the less. . . . Any man's death diminishes me, because I am involved in mankind. Therefore, never send [to know] for whom the bell tolls; it tolls for thee."[2] Donne reminds us that we are all connected and affected by each other through bonds of humanity, something that sick people and their neighbors can easily forget. But he also insists that each person's illness or death has a meaning and imperative for the larger community. "The bell tolls for thee," he wrote from his sickbed, not "me." This sense that one's illness is not just a private problem, a matter of personal fault or responsibility, but a collective one shared by all, is something that sick people often come to on their own.

I remember the day that notion first took form in my mind. A good friend of mine who works for an organization that protects the waterways of northern New Mexico came by to visit after work. As we sat on the porch swing drinking lemonade, she told me that the Red River, a tributary of the Rio Grande, had become so polluted from an upstream mine it was turning a milky Windex-blue color, and the local fishermen were calling it "Dead River," because the fish were dying. I, in turn, told her what I had recently learned, that my intestines were so congested with an overgrowth of parasites and candida that my body could barely extract nourishment from the food I ate. In the silence that fell between us, we both understood that my illness and the contamination of the Red River were strangely related. "Isn't it interesting," my friend pondered, to the slow rhythm of our swinging, "as the waters of the earth become increasingly polluted, millions of people are getting sick and dying from immune disorders." Yes, I thought, the earth is suffering and we are her symptoms.

The understanding that an individual's illness may be part of a greater disease or design is not new, even to Western thinking. The ancient Greeks believed that illness could result from the crimes of one's ancestors, or the transgressions of a whole people, as well as personal fault. Early Jews and Christians understood, from the biblical story of Adam and Eve, that the sufferings which afflict people, including illness, are the results or wages of an original sin that is not individual, but shared by all. And Renaissance physicians, informed by the hermetic doctrines of ancient Egypt, believed that the events that occur in the small world of our bodies reflect what is happening in the larger world of our universe; so it was often said: "As above, so below." All understood that the welfare of an individual is shaped by forces that extend throughout space and time, an awareness that is shared by many indigenous peoples to this day.

THE WEB OF LIFE

Indigenous peoples commonly regard the illness of an individual to be symptomatic of disharmony in the cosmic order, an indication that some violation of nature has occurred, which has not been righted; therefore someone is sick, the rains do not come, or people fight among themselves. This understanding is predicated upon the recognition that all things are sacred, necessary, and related in the great circle or web of life. Since nothing exists in isolation, and everything depends upon everything else, one cannot disturb any element of nature without upsetting the rest. For this reason, indigenous peoples insist that we are obliged as human beings to live in ways that sustain all life. Chief Seattle articulated this understanding eloquently in 1854, in his reply to President Pierce's offer to buy land from the Salish tribes of the Pacific Northwest: "The earth does not belong to man; man belongs to the earth. This we know. All things are connected like the blood which unites one family. . . . Man did not weave the web of life; he is merely a strand in it. Whatever he does to the web, he does to himself."[3] In other words, as an elderly Mohawk woman told a Quebec policeman during protests in 1990, "If you shoot me, you're shooting your mother and your grandmother, because that's who I am."

In this web of life, there are not only physical connections and dependencies among all things, but spiritual ones as well. These are affinities or correspondences, ties of kinship, totem, or clan, that align certain people with certain animals, plants, minerals, seasons, stars, landforms, ancestor spirits, etc., in bonds of identity and responsibility. For example, all turtles, and all representations of turtles in clay, paint, or ritual, the people who belong to turtle clans, the places turtles lay their eggs, and the times of year they hatch, all partake of an essential "turtleness," just as all mothers embody aspects of the universal mother. A disturbance in one member of the "family" is reflected, simultaneously, in all the others. If one mother is killed, all mothers are diminished; if a watershed is polluted, one may also find an increase in alcoholism, dry winters, an absence of bluebirds come spring—or an epidemic of CFIDS. When this happens, it is time to call on the ancestors for help.

In the cosmologies of most indigenous peoples, the visible world of people, plants, and animals is interpenetrated by an invisible world of ancestors and spirits, who function to uphold and enforce the laws or natural ways that keep all things in balance. Tribal cultures develop customs and rules to guide "Earth Surface People" (as the Diné or Navajo call us) in the ways of harmonious living, so as not to antagonize the "Holy People" (another Diné term). These traditions define and protect the delicate ecology of visible and invisible worlds that sustain life; people follow them because the world depends upon them to do so. They know that an intentional—or unintentional—violation of those rules could offend the ancestors and bring harm upon their families, communities, or the cosmos itself for generations to come. That is why so many healing ceremonies of indigenous peoples, from the African Yoruba to the Arctic Inuit, call upon the entire community to make prayers and offerings to appease the Holy People and restore harmony to their world.

Not long ago I attended hearings before the New Mexico state engineer regarding a water rights transfer for a proposed resort development in northern New Mexico. A representative from a neighboring Indian pueblo—a dignified older man who spoke in his native tongue, while an interpreter translated—testified that if the water for that development were to be pumped from the aquifer, the water table beneath a small wetlands area on the pueblo would be lowered, drying up sacred springs, clays, and herbs traditionally used by Indians along the Rio Grande for ritual purposes. At one point the lawyer representing the developers pointed out that the state engineer is required to consider the welfare of *all* state residents, not just one small community, to which the pueblo spokesman simply responded: "Our prayers are for the whole world."

It is this invisible dimension of reality, in which all people and things are connected and sustained by spiritual forces, that the scientific materialism of recent centuries cannot see, in fact refuses to see. This shortsightedness, which is peculiar to white, Western civilization, limits our understanding of health and illness and our ability to affect them. As Fritjof Capra noted, "the problems biologists cannot solve today, apparently because of their narrow, fragmented approach, all seem to be related to the function of living systems as wholes and to their interactions with their environment"—how we develop as embryos, for example, and breathe, digest, heal wounds, regulate body temperature, and focus attention—"precisely the functions that are crucial for the organism's health."[4]

The scientific search for a single physical cause or "pathogen" in disease ignores the physical, social, and spiritual contexts that give rise to health and disease. Even Louis Pasteur, who is credited with developing the germ theory of disease, was intensely interested in what he called "the terrain," the internal and external environments or ecology of the organism. Shortly before his death, Pasteur wrote: "If I were to undertake new studies of the silkworm diseases, I would direct my effort to the environmental conditions that increase their vigor and resistance."

Finally, some one hundred years later, medical researchers are beginning to do just that. The extraordinary microscopic technology of modern medicine is revealing and demonstrating the invisible interconnections that ancient and native peoples have always recognized. Biochemists, for example, have discovered the presence of chemical transmitters, called neuropeptides, that join our brain, glands, and immune systems in a network of communication between body and mind. Their presence demonstrates a physiological basis for what is commonly known as our "sixth sense"—the wisdom of our bodies—effectively eradicating boundaries between mind, body, and soul that many Westerners had come to assume. They also explain how emotional states can affect physical health, how someone can die of a broken heart, or survive against all odds by telling the truth. To my thinking, one of the most intriguing facts about neuropeptides is that they have been found in identical formulations in all forms of life, from protozoa to mice to people; they may provide a molecular basis for communication between the species, the ways in which we commune and commiserate with our surroundings without even knowing it. With neuropeptides in mind, I can easily imagine how prayers can ripple through the realms of nature to benefit the entire world.

Microbiologists, in turn, have discovered that microbes, including known pathogens such as viruses and bacteria, are commonly present in the tissues of healthy individuals; in fact, they exist in a delicate equilibrium and partnership with higher forms of life. Many microbes, such as intestinal bacteria, serve useful and necessary functions under normal conditions, but they can cause toxic reactions and even death under other conditions. Apparently, bacteria and viruses are neither good nor bad, life-sustaining nor life-destroying, in and of themselves; diseases arise only when the ecological equilibrium between microbe and man is disturbed, which can occur under many influences, such as drug use, chemical or radiation exposure, adverse working or living conditions, malnutrition, emotional stress, or social disruption. Even the AIDS virus, commonly thought to be the most deadly known to humankind, can infect an individual without leading to disease, as thousands of healthy HIV-positive individuals can attest. For this reason, some AIDS researchers and activists are beginning to explore the role of other risk factors, such as the use of recreational drugs and prescribed antibiotics, malnutrition, and the absence of viable emotional support systems. These discoveries turn our attention to relationships—between people and between species—and to notions of balance and imbalance, which are the primary concerns of indigenous peoples in addressing illness.

It is evident, from the teachings of many indigenous peoples and some of the more recent discoveries of medical science, that the presence of disease reflects a larger disorder, a disruption of the system of checks and balances that sustains life, a tear in the cosmic web. It may also reflect the efforts of that encompassing system to mend itself; for transformation, whether it manifests as a forest fire or the fever of cholera, is the primary process that relates all aspects of nature to one another. It is always at work to reorder an imbalanced world.

Illness provides an impressive example of transformation at work, precisely because the physiological substratum of our body-mind unity is intimately connected, even identified, with the invisible workings of nature, that mythic underworld in which all things are related and continually created. But how does it work? How does the mining of uranium in northern Arizona relate to the rising incidence of leukemia throughout the United States, as Hopi elders have suggested? And why do some people get sick while others do not? I brought these questions to a teacher of mine, Dr. Pat Sargent, and she directed me to the myths of the ancient Greeks for an understanding of the nature of shame. Her study of shame in the context of natural and political orders has illuminated my understanding of my own illness, and of the collective ills we must all confront.[5]

THE DYNAMICS OF SHAME AND SCAPEGOATING

Pre-hellenic Greeks personified the natural way, order, or balance of all things as the Goddess Dike, also known as Themis. Dike represented the way of each and every plant, animal, and human being on the face of the earth, but also the way of that great animal, the Universe, which encompasses all these beings and shows its face in the changing seasons, the rising and falling of vegetation, and the waxing and waning of the moon. Dike belonged to the underworld and was often pictured with a wheel, in the recognition that change is always at work to maintain an ever-fluctuating, live and breathing natural order. Later Dike became associated with the moral effort we human beings make to bring ourselves into accordance with the natural way or order, and came to represent the principles of Right and Justice.

The Greeks understood that whenever the natural order of Dike was violated, the powers of righteous anger (Nemesis) and shame (Aidos) would be invoked, so that wrongs might be righted and the single strand rewoven into the web. Aidos, who was pictured as a butterfly, represented the sense of reverence for life that holds us back from wrongdoing and the sense of shame we feel in the presence of injustice. Concentration camp survivor Primo Levi described this latter form of Aidos as "the shame which the just man experiences when confronted by a crime committed by another, and he feels remorse because of its existence, because of its having been irrevocably introduced into the world of living things, and because his will has proven nonexistent or feeble and was incapable of putting up a good defense."[6] Originally, shame carried a sense of the sacred, that great Mystery which infuses all life, instilling a healthy respect, reverence, and humility. It served to remind us human beings, so prone to hubris, that we are not God, that we have made and will make mistakes. It allowed us to acknowledge our mistakes and prompted us to remedy them to the best of our abilities. To the Greek understanding, shame was the antidote for human hubris, the remedy for wrongdoing, our means of mending the web.

Hesiod, the Greek poet who wrote the history of the world during the eighth century B.C., predicted that there would come a time during the age of iron, our current age, when people would become so depraved that Aidos and Nemesis would depart for the heavens and leave us to our own undoing. When that time arrives, he wrote, "A father will not be in harmony with his children nor his children with him, nor guest with host, nor friend with friend, and a brother will not be loved as formerly. One will destroy the city of another. No esteem will exist for the one who is true to an oath or just or good; rather men will praise the arrogance and evil of the wicked. Justice will be might and shame will not exist. . . . Then Aidos and Nemesis both will forsake mankind and go, their beautiful forms shrouded in white, from the wide earth to Olympus among the company of the gods . . . and there will be no defense against evil."[7]

Hesiod made it clear that when the natural bonds between people are broken and violence becomes the way of the day, we will lose our capacity to feel righteous anger and shame, and so lack protection from evil, the results of wrongdoing in our world. That is when the natural law of Dike is replaced by the social law of man, which further disrupts our ability to perceive the natural order and respond accordingly.

Apparently, that time has come. After centuries of institutionalized violence, during which the gods and goddesses of the natural way have been buried and replaced by the laws of political orders, shame has been split from its sacred roots and function. Aidos has left the earth, but her shadow persists as a more toxic shame—the pervasive, unrelenting sense of being wrong or bad, unworthy or unfit as a human being—that afflicts so many sensitive, abused, or oppressed peoples.

Psychologists have made some interesting observations about the nature and origins of "toxic" shame, many of which corroborate Hesiod's prophecies. Gershen Kaufman, author of *Shame: The Power of Caring,* pointed out that shame is generated whenever the bonds of trust are broken (as Hesiod predicted) between significant others, such as family members, friends, or lovers, even teachers and students. This occurs, he explained, when someone does not acknowledge or respond to the needs of intimate others and so violates their personhood, as commonly occurs in situations of abuse, abandonment, or prejudice. Autonomic physiological responses like blushing, sweating, or shaking betray the presence of shame and teach us that shame touches and affects very deep layers of the body-mind where disease originates. Apologies, which would be prompted by Aidos if we could feel the touch of her wings, can remedy the situation and restore trust if the behaviors are discontinued, but when apologies are not forthcoming and the behaviors continue, the person who has been violated—or even witnessed the violation of another—will begin to internalize the shame and perpetuate the abuse against themselves or others.

The experience of profound shame is excruciating, so unbearable that we usually develop ways to compensate and defend ourselves. We disown the rejected parts of ourselves—our needs, emotions, or perceptions that were painfully exposed in shaming incidents—and cultivate false selves to protect ourselves and please others. In so doing, we lose the ability to trust our experience and relate empathically, and come to rely upon external standards of performance, collective ideals, to guide our actions. In a culture of shame, the highest authority is a good reputation, not a good conscience; respectability replaces responsibility.

We also resort to stances of contempt or arrogance, moralizing or caretaking, in our efforts to evade the agony of shame; we are also likely to develop compulsions, addictions, and other repetitive, self-destructive behaviors. As we deny our own feelings and needs, we cannot acknowledge or respond appropriately to those of others; in fact, we are likely to treat others in exactly the same ways we have been treated and continue to treat ourselves. Shame begets shame, in a vicious, self-perpetuating cycle of lies and violence.

At this point shame rarely lands on the shoulders of those who commit the transgressions: the corporate polluters, wife beaters, or keepers of apartheid, and all of us who disregard the life of another, acting as if we were something apart and above the people, animals, and landforms surrounding us. We, the inheritors of white Western civilization, are so convinced of our separateness and superiority, so numb to our own original pain, that we inflict upon others what we cannot feel in the name of practicality, progress, and even love. Without Aidos to guide us, we cannot accept the shame and responsibility of our actions or correct our behaviors. As a result, shame floats free of the "shameless" trespassers and lands upon the trespassed, those who are treated shamefully—the women, children, and old people, the underclassed, outcast, and oppressed—who come to manifest the symptoms of distress and disease, becoming the sacrifices. Shame is highly contagious in these ways; I have come to think of it as the psychological equivalent of free-floating viruses and bacteria.

Sarah Pirtle, whose son was born with multiple defects because her mother had taken DES, described the contagious nature of shame from her experience: "When my mother learned she had taken DES she was ashamed. She felt tremendous guilt. Then when my son Ryan was born, she couldn't stand hearing the updates on whether or not he was surviving. She felt his problems were her fault. What a travesty! Here's my mother simply following the prescriptions the doctor gave her, and *she's* feeling guilty. The doctor isn't feeling guilty. The drug company isn't feeling guilty. . . . It's like a spell cast over the victim."[8]

Shame is further instilled and institutionalized with blame, the finding of personal fault in the victim, by those who are anxious to deny their part of the responsibility: family members, friends and neighbors, professionals, and politicians. So the identified child in a disturbed family is sent to the psychiatrist to treat "his" problem, welfare recipients are accused of being lazy and denied adequate support, child care, or job opportunities, and gay men are blamed and ostracized for the rise of AIDS. AIDS is a good case in point, because public attitudes of fear, hostility, and homophobia have brought the disease to epidemic proportions; and the ones who suffer most from these cultural attitudes are the ones who are dying, sacrifices to a collective illness, a shame that belongs to all of us.

These are the dynamics of scapegoating, in which a community faced with its own imperfections and failings shifts the blame onto some of its members, who are then identified with evil or wrongdoing, and exiled or punished so that the remaining members can feel exonerated, and the communal mores can be justified and reinforced. Here we find the toxic shadow of Nemesis, the Greek goddess of righteous anger, who fled the earth with Aidos. In blaming the sick—or the poor, or anyone else who has met with misfortune or injustice—scapegoaters feel lighter, freer, stronger, and safer from the afflictions of life, relieved of the burden of their own fears, mistakes, and misgivings. The scapegoated, on the other hand, feel inferior, heavy, guilty, and vulnerable, for they are burdened with the unanswered questions, the shame and shadow of the collective. While we all partake of both sides of this dynamic at various points and places in our lives, those primarily identified with the scapegoat role acknowledge and suffer the wounds we all share, and come to manifest the symptoms: ruptures of psyche and body.

For this reason, Yaël Bethiem, who lives with a painful, disabling disease, relates her illness to the fact that the Earth is a "living being that is hurting and polluted," wondering if sick and disabled people like herself might be the Earth's "random nerve cells" calling our attention to her distress.[9] In a similar fashion, many people with CFIDS, environmental sensitivity, and cancer—immune disorders that have reached epidemic proportions in recent years—liken themselves to the canaries in the coal mines, whose sufferings provide evidence that we have made our world so toxic as to be unlivable. As Audre Lorde explained, "I am a scar, a report from the front lines. . . . For me, my [mastectomy] scars are an honorable reminder that I may be a casualty in the cosmic war against radiation, animal fat, air pollution, McDonald's hamburgers, and Red Dye #2."[10]

In ancient times, scapegoat rituals were performed to appease the anger of the underworld gods for the inevitable and sometimes unwitting transgressions of humankind, so the community of life could be healed and renewed. Even though the practice of scapegoating has been torn from its sacred roots, trivialized, and distorted, many sick people still carry the sense that their affliction is serving some greater purpose beyond themselves. As one man with sleeping sickness told his doctor: "I am a living candle. I am consumed that you may learn. New things will be seen in the light of my suffering." While it is possible to overdo our identification with collective responsibilities, and compensate for our shame by feeling superior, as though "chosen" to redeem others, it is still true that all our lives affect and are affected by all others. Perhaps that is why many sick people are horrified at the thought that their stories might be left untold, their sufferings forgotten and so wasted by people too busy, blinded, or righteous to hear the bell toll for them.

Even those who do not have the sense that their illnesses redeem or renew anything for anyone else often recognize that they are part of a larger system of checks and balances that holds our universe together and in balance. Nancy Mairs, who is crippled with multiple sclerosis, wrote: "If I could make a cosmic deal [and be relieved of MS], who would I put in my place?"[11] When I told a close friend of mine, a gay man who has miraculously escaped HIV infection, that I thought I might be dying, his immediate response, without thinking, was: "You got sick instead of me."

Transpersonal psychologist Ken Wilber, who supported his wife Treya through her life and death with cancer and then developed CFIDS himself, understands illness in the context of karma—the notion that all actions bear fruits that must be reaped at some time. "If you have killed someone in a past life," Wilber explained, "that killing, because it is an ontological offense against the moral grain of the universe, is going to have a correspondingly bad effect on the structure of your very soul. It will come to a retributive fruition, and you will pay—usually, it is said, by a short life riddled with disease and illness." However, he continued, others may pay that price, because karma is collective as well as individual. "If you end up in Treblinka or Dachau, it's not necessarily only, or even predominantly, your bad karma. It's mostly Hitler's and Himmler's and Heydrich's. If major industries dump carcinogenic toxins into your environment and you get cancer, it's not primarily your bad karma. It's theirs."[12] In fact, many Buddhist scholars insist that it is incorrect to speak of "my" karma or "your" karma, since notions of mine and yours belong to the illusory sense of individual self we call ego. In the end, there is only karma, the psychic inheritance and accumulation of mankind's actions, some of which, I suspect, can only be expressed and experienced by the variations of health and illness.

BLOOD GUILT

Arnold Mindell once observed that many sick and dying people "dream their body problems are centuries old."[13] I had such a dream, several in fact, during the worst year of my illness. The first one that caught my attention was the dream in which my doctor found the semen of the man who molested me as a child in my saliva and told me that I could not be free until it was out. As the dream continued, my doctor handed me a form to fill out about my illness which included several questions about family history and genetics. At first the questions seemed irrelevant, but after answering them, I began to suspect there was more to this business of genes and ancestry than I had realized. That dream was followed by others about my ancestors, who settled in central Minnesota in the mid 1800s, when the local native peoples (the woodland Sioux, who belonged to the federation of tribes known as the Dakota) were being driven from the land that had fed them for centuries. In one of those dreams, the basement walls of my grandmother's house next door were painted like a mural with images of imperialism: German soldiers marching in unison, Spanish conquistadors on horseback with shining helmets, and more.

As a result of these dreams, I became preoccupied with figuring out how my ancestors had acquired the land I grew up on. My father, the family historian, told me that my great-great-grandfather bought it from another white man, who, in turn, had received it from the state of Minnesota after the Treaty of Traverse des Sioux in 1851, but something continued to bother me about those events, and I began to wonder if they had anything to do with my illness. After discussing the matter with my counselor, I decided to consult a shaman, since shamans are specially trained to discern the far-reaching lines of causation in illness.

When I met with the shaman a few weeks later, he asked me about the symptoms of my illness, my family history (the questions from my dream!), and my dreams. Then he looked into his bundle to see the truth of the matter, and said: "You are a sacrifice dying so that others may live . . . we would not call you sick, but wounded." He explained that there were several factors involved with my illness, one of which had to do with what happened when my ancestors settled on Indian land in Minnesota. Apparently, the particular band of Sioux who lived in that area had been there for many generations, unlike other Minnesota tribes who were more nomadic by nature. They were attached to that land, which fed them well and held the bones of their ancestors; as a result, many sickened, starved, or froze to death in the winters that followed their removal. Those deaths, the shaman explained, made a "big gash in the land, and your body is the wound."

Something like a curse, or requirement, was laid upon my family at that time, that each generation would get smaller and smaller until the name died out, unless a sacrifice was made. The shaman told me that if I did not wish to be that sacrifice, I should honor the people who died and make offerings to them, so that the ill will generated by that tragedy could be transformed into benevolence. He helped me to do that honoring a month later, and ever since I have felt relieved of a certain heaviness, the sense that I did not deserve to be alive, that has been with me as long as I can remember. When I came home that night, I announced to my lover, "I know I am going to get well."

While getting well has turned out to be a very complicated process that requires much more of me than I could have imagined at the time, the work I did with the shaman enabled me to turn the tide of my illness away from death and back toward life so that I could go on to address the other factors that were implicated in my demise.

When I think of what happened in the woodlands of Minnesota, almost one hundred years before my birth, I go in my mind to the tip of a small peninsula called Spirit Knob that juts out into Lake Minnetonka less than a mile from where I was raised. I used to walk the trail through the woods, past my grandmother's house and down to the lake, where the path nearly died out in a tangle of cedar before it arrived at the point, and stand there on a rock surrounded by water on three sides as far as the eye could see. There I imagine the fierce and bearded countenance of my great-great-grandfather, Samuel C. Gale, standing in a black suit and buttoned bow tie, looking out across the waters.

Samuel Gale was an ambitious, self-made man who found his fortune on the frontier. Raised in Massachusetts, he apprenticed to a tanner at the age of eleven, educated himself from books at the public library, and eventually worked his way through Yale University. In 1857 he moved to Minneapolis, joining the flood of white settlers who pushed into Indian country after the woodland Sioux surrendered nine-tenths of their land (some thirty-five million acres) in the treaties of Traverse des Sioux and Mendota in 1851. Though trained as a lawyer, Gale opened a real estate and loan office and became a rich man by buying and selling huge tracts of land that had once been the home of the Sioux. One day, so the family story goes, he went to look at a piece of land west of Minneapolis on the shores of Lake Minnetonka; it was spring, the sun was shining, violets were blooming, and he was smitten. He bought the land that week and later built a summer home on it, to become one of the first whites to settle in the area.

It is hard to figure out exactly what transpired on that land during the turbulent years of Indian-white conflict in Minnesota. History books, which are inevitably written by the conquerors, tend to gloss over the details of conquest and erase the peoples who were conquered. However, a few facts have emerged from my study. I have learned that the handful of Sioux chiefs who signed the treaties of Traverse des Sioux and Mendota did not represent all the tribes living in the territory negotiated. One of those chiefs, Red Iron of the Sisseton Sioux, told Governor Ramsey the following year: "When we signed the treaty the traders threw a blanket over our faces and darkened our eyes, and made us sign papers which we did not understand, and which were not explained or read to us."[14] In the year that followed, the United States government refused to deliver most of the money and provisions it had promised in the treaties. The Sioux were crowded into a small reservation along the Minnesota River, denied access to their traditional hunting and gathering grounds, and left to starve. When a small band of Sioux revolted in 1862, stealing food and attacking white settlements, the government retaliated with military force, using the opportunity to drive the Indians out of Minnesota.

Three years later, my great-great-grandfather took an interest in the land on Lake Minnetonka. While most of the land he bought there had already passed through the hands of one or two other white men since the Treaty of Traverse des Sioux, one small piece of it—Spirit Knob—had not; Samuel Gale acquired that peninsula directly from the government in 1865, after the Sioux Uprising. I think it is fair to assume that the Indians who lived in the area did not willingly relinquish that land, especially since early white visitors found signs of Sioux worship on the point, suggesting that Spirit Knob was a sacred site used for ceremonial purposes. While the history books often maintain that the Sioux went west to the Dakotas or north to Canada after the war, the shaman told me that the particular tribe who lived in that area did not abandon their ancestral home ground; they stayed in the forests nearby for quite some time, holding vigil. My great-great-grandfather probably saw their campfires flickering across the lake by night, for his granddaughter, my grandmother, remembered seeing them as a child.

If Samuel Gale saw those fires or noticed the painted rocks on Spirit Knob, I doubt that he dwelled for very long on the events that prompted the Indians to leave. After all, he had left his own past behind and risen far beyond it, and he would have had no way to understand how indigenous peoples, like the Native Americans, are sustained by the land they inherit and caretake. Given his Puritan zeal and all that he stood to gain from the affair, it is likely that he saw nothing unjust in the actions white settlers took to drive the so-called pagan savages from the land. In the end, it does not matter, for regardless of the extent of his guilt or innocence, a piece of the toll of that unjust war landed on his shoulders and those of his family and descendants.

Yes, the sins of the fathers are visited upon the children, and continue onto the seventh generation, as biblical and Native American traditions claim. The Bible calls it "blood guilt"; psychologists name it "inherited shame," the "genealogical shadow," or simply the "white shadow," and explain that it most often occurs in families or communities where there are silences, secrets, and unanswered questions surrounding traumatic events in the past, such as suicides, bankruptcies, betrayals, thefts, pregnancies, and wars. "The old instinct," wrote Laguna author Leslie Marmon Silko in her novel about healing, *Ceremony*, "would be to gather the feelings and opinions [about the trauma] that were scattered through the village, to gather them like willow twigs and tie them into a single prayer bundle that would bring peace to all of them. But now [years later] the feelings were twisted, tangled roots, and all the names for the source of this growth were buried . . . out of reach. There would be no peace and the people would have no rest until the entanglement had been unwound to the source."[15] When events remain unresolved, they persist to haunt future generations like a ghost—the proverbial family skeleton.

Mary Winfrey Trautmann described one such family skeleton that came to haunt her while her daughter was struggling with leukemia. Apparently, when Trautmann was five years old, her pregnant aunt fell—or was pushed by Trautmann's manic-depressive mother—down the basement stairs and lost the child she was carrying. "When the aunt, who simply refused to speak of the incident," wrote Trautmann, "left our house for good, the adults entered into a conspiracy of silence. My father happened to be absent that February day. He was never told. My mother cannot remember the event; it occupies a mysterious bleakness in her mind. If bitterness festers in anyone, it rankles in silence. But we all know the aunt never became pregnant again. . . ."

When her daughter developed leukemia, Trautmann suddenly remembered this incident with remorse, as the family member, who was a child at the time, who carried the shame for everyone involved. It occurred to her that her aunt (who had since died) "might want my child now. Because I too abandoned her, I may now be compelled to suffer as she did, learn what she learned." Trautmann decided to "establish some kind of peace" with her aunt; she spontaneously and instinctively gathered an armful of flowers, took them to the top of a hill, and laid them down as an offering before the great expanses of earth and sky. Later she noted, in reference to the hold this family skeleton had upon her, "the claws have receded."[16]

It is not uncommon for the poisons of inherited shame to manifest in serious illness. Metaphysician Alice Bailey asserted in her treatise on esoteric healing that "inheritance . . . those tainted streams of energy which are of group origin" is the most common cause of disease.[17] Dr. Deepak Chopra explained how this can be when he noted that the immune system has incredible powers of memory; it "knows all our secrets, all our sorrows. It knows why a mother who has lost a child can die of grief. . . ." If choice exists in the creation of illness, he continued, it "takes place below the level of conscious thoughts," where the "ghosts of memory" reside.[18]

I suspect that the psyches and bodies of twentieth-century Americans are crowded and overflowing with these ghosts of memory so implicated in disease, because we as a people are so oriented toward progress and eager to escape the burdens and complications of continuity. It is the American way (as exemplified by my ancestors, but also by my own life) to leave one's home and past behind to start a new life on the great frontier, leaving a terrible—and toxic—trail of unfinished business.

Perhaps that is why survivors of all kinds so often insist upon remembering the dead and forgotten, and why descendants of the Sioux Indians who survived the Wounded Knee Massacre of 1890 journeyed by foot and by horseback to the grave site one hundred years later, across hundreds of miles through subzero temperatures, to offer prayers, burn sage, and receive the apology of South Dakota Governor George Mickelson. The Sioux, like many other tribes, have repeatedly asked for an apology from the United States government for the atrocities of the past in the recognition that our lives and well-being, as red and white peoples, depend upon the mending of these wounds.

The Indo-European root for the word "cure," *kios*, means to sorrow for something,[19] and I have yet to meet a sick person who doesn't sorrow deeply for something: the breakdown of a marriage, an early death in the family, or the nameless innocents slaughtered in war. A good friend of mine who came down with CFIDS after visiting Nicaragua says it broke her heart to see how our government is destroying that country, and that is why she is sick. Shame carriers, like my friend, smell something rotten and look for the corpse in order to bury it properly, to return the world to order and balance. They point to the atrocities we have grown accustomed to and cry out: "There's been a murder!" to waken us from the slumber of our hardened hearts, the illusions of normalcy. So my friend persists in speaking and writing about the crimes our government perpetuates in Central America. I believe that the force of her pain, horror, and grief, her simple ability to feel the losses we all share and the underlying connections that inform them, helps to heal our broken world, even though it is also implicated in her illness.

Our bodies bear the untold lessons and scars of history. As we suffer our wounds in the extremities of illness, they become our offerings, our means of realizing and remembering what is right, what is needed, to bring our lives and our world back into balance. "Consciously lived suffering," wrote Jungian analyst Marie-Louise von Franz, "has a redeeming effect upon the past and future of mankind, an effect which is exerted invisibly from the Beyond."[20] Illness must be understood in the context of the shared history of a people; it is dangerous to personalize it as "my" fault. It is another one of those curious paradoxes of illness that something so intensely private should be so collective in origin and effects.

8

MYTHOLOGY AND THE DARK HEART OF HEALING

Shall I tell you how many
months I have been ill?
And that I have learned many
new routes into our
endless curiosity about
existence. How the sharpest pain
takes you like a lover, leaves
no room for any other desire
except absence. How what is more subtle
erodes   leaves you
suspended somewhere
outside what you have always
called real.
. . .
At the center of
all my sorrows
I have felt a presence
that was not mine alone.

—Susan Griffin[1]

There are moments in the midst of illness when we lean over the brink, as if drawn by some invisible force, into that place beyond, where all things begin and end; I think of it as that tiny gap, which is also a yawning chasm, that exists between life and death, form and formlessness. Oliver Sacks called it a "limbo" between worlds; Max Lerner likened it to the "darkness and void of the opening lines of Genesis." It is the primal void, unfathomably deep, dark and still, and yet it also moves, some say, like a whirlpool or whirlwind. Momentous transactions occur in this vortex of empty space, which we can only call healing. Sacks wrote that during the "twelve timeless days" of his stay in limbo, what began as a "hideous and unspeakable hell" turned into "something utterly, mysteriously different—a night no longer abominable and dark, but radiant, with a light above sense—and with this, a curious, paradoxical joy. . . ."[2] The experience, he wrote, gave new meaning to John Donne's cryptic lines: "I am rebegot of Absence, Darkness, Death; things which are not."

Illness is not the only route to this invisible underworld that informs the perilous ground we walk upon as human beings; all sorts of crises, humiliations, and woundings can take us there. But illness is one of the most reliable routes, simply because it is engineered by the strange and intractable forces of physical life, and if we are ever to understand the mysteries of healing, it behooves us to acquaint ourselves with the powers of the deep, that mysterious Presence that is found amid "Absence, Darkness, Death."

THE INSULTED GODDESSES OF THE DEEP

Our first encounters with the deep are terrifying, for we feel ourselves to be caught—like the fly in a spider's web—in the clutch of vast cosmic processes beyond our control and understanding. Life takes on the quality of a nightmare. We try to resist and escape, but inevitably we are caught, broken, and crushed by illness, as if devoured by some great monster (a "huge grizzly bear," wrote Denton Welch), or ground to a pulp in the wheels of a merciless machine ("the grim grindstone of physical pain," as Alice James described it).

This "grim grindstone" has been called the black heart of nature, the destructive/transformative side of the cosmic will; it is the energy of big bangs and black holes, rotting apples and sprouting acorns, digestion and gestation. These are the blind, autonomic forces of physical life to which we all submit. In illness they seem to run amok in a frenzy of chaos, a fury of destruction; tumors grow silently and secretly like mushrooms from the trunk of a tree, parasites invade and proliferate like sweeping plagues of locusts, and appendixes burst with the unexpected fury of volcanoes—and it all occurs without our knowledge or consent, like a "raging river," as one cancer survivor noted.

Ancient and tribal peoples have often recognized a face in this raging river, the face of a dark, primordial, death-wielding, and life-giving goddess of the underworld, variously known as Hecate, Erishkegal, Coatlicue, Cerridwen, Oya, Kali, and other names.[3] In her novel about healing, *The Salt-Eaters,* Toni Cade Bambara simply called her the "mud mother" who resides in an ancient, ancestral cave awaiting the inevitable return of the sick and the haunted who seek restoration, noting "there was no escaping the calling, the caves, the mud mothers . . . No escape."[4] Laura Chester named her the "Hag," explaining that she was "part fury and part grace."

The Hag embodies the law, or maw, of ruthless necessity, the regulatory force of nature, what might be called "cosmic justice"; on a personal level, we experience her presence as fate or destiny, and the physical limits and requirements of our living—all of which become so painfully evident in illness. Serious illnesses, physical or mental, could be described as encounters with the Hag; as Chicana author Gloria Anzaldúa noted, "when pain, suffering and the advent of death become intolerable . . . Coatlicue, the Earth, opens and plunges us into its maw, devours us."[5]

White Westerners are not well acquainted with the Hag, since she was banished from our world and consciousness during the enlightenment of the eighteenth century. Even though we have forgotten her, she has not forgotten us; she persists as the wicked witch in our dreams and fairy tales—those relics of ancestral memory—and in our fears of ruthless women, devouring mothers, and dark peoples. As the myths and teachings of many indigenous peoples attest, the Hag continues to guard the boundaries of natural law and to retaliate with a vengeance when they are not respected for whatever reason, be it ignorance, pride, or simple disregard. Nor will she tolerate being forgotten, as Albert Kreinheder discovered one night while investigating his arthritic pain. He wrote:

> I was taking 24 aspirins a day. The dry bones were grating against each other and the pain was awesome . . . when I felt I could stand it no longer, I spoke to the pain:
>
> ME: You hold me tight in your grip and do not let me go. . . . Why? Why are you here?
>
> PAIN: I am here to get your attention. I make known my presence. I have a power beyond your power. My will surpasses yours. You cannot prevail over me, but I can easily prevail over you.
>
> ME: But why must you show me this power and destroy me with it?
>
> PAIN: I show you because I will no longer let you disregard me. You can no longer treat me as if I am not. You will know my power, and you will humble yourself before me. I am the first of all things, and all things spring from me, and without me there is nothing. I want you to see me and feel me and hear me and to bring to me the best of yourself . . . out of this will come many good things.[6]

As Kreinheder discovered, the Hag is bitter and brooding; she is easily insulted, never forgets, and demands an offering, a sacrifice, to set things straight. I suspect that is where illness comes in—or my illness, at least—for the shaman I consulted when I got sick told me that the goddess of the sea who lives in my womb is angry and insulted and must be appeased.

Perhaps that is why two of these insulted underworld goddesses—Tlalteuctli of Meso-American traditions, and Takánakapsâluk of the Arctic Inuit Indians, both of which abide on this continent—have been very close to me since I have been sick, helping me to understand the dark truths of illness: the painful sacrifices and sacred transactions that occur in its midst. Since these goddesses are based in nonliterate cultures quite foreign to my own, I cannot presume to know them as they are known by the peoples who honor them ritually; what follows must be understood as my own imaginative rendering of their stories and teachings, portrayed through the filter of my own needs and purposes. For the only way I can evoke and describe this ultimately ineffable dark heart of the universe, that black hole that opens up in illness, and begin to address the question of healing that rises from its center, is through storytelling: the telling of my dreams, the stories of the goddesses, my experiences and those of other sick people.

THE UNENDING CRAVING FOR HEARTS

When I was getting sick, but did not know it, I had a dream that unnerved me for quite some time. It was a simple dream, not much more than an image: I was holding hands with a very competent, worldly twin sister. She had been murdered, chopped into pieces, and spread all around the room, only I was so young and unaware—

barely able to see—that I did not know it. I just felt a dawning sense of dread and on-my-ownness as I sat on my bed, holding one of her fingers in mine.

In retrospect, this dream seems to predict my illness, the death and destruction of my competent, able-bodied worldliness through the months of exhaustion, fevers, muscle weakness, and memory loss that were to follow. (That feeling I had in the dream, of being young and ignorant, without the confidence of sure knowledge, is close to me still.) But at the time I had no way of knowing what was to come, and the feelings and images of the dream haunted me for several days . . . until I encountered the story of Tlalteuctli. It was just a few sentences in a mythology book, but with those words, her almighty presence leaped off the page and into my world.

Tlalteuctli is one of the oldest deities of the Nahuatl, pre-Aztec peoples of Mexico; she was known as the "great earth monster" who thrashed about in the churning waters of primordial chaos. Some sources describe her as a colossal toad with unblinking eyes and snapping jaws at every joint, and centipedes, scorpions, spiders, and serpents slithering through her hair.[7] Her story, which is a story about creation, has consistently intrigued me, alternately frightened and comforted me, throughout the course of my illness. This is how it goes: One day, as Tlalteuctli was walking alone on the primordial waters, she was assaulted by the gods of light and dark—Quetzalcoatl, the Plumed Serpent, and his twin brother Tezcatlipoca, the Smoking Mirror. They grabbed her by the hands and feet and ripped her apart. Her lower part rose to form the heavens, and the upper half descended to become the Earth. The gods then fashioned all the features and fruits of the earth that people need to live from her body parts. From her hair they made trees, flowers, and grass; from her eyes, springs and little caves; from her shoulders, the mountains, and so on. That is how the world as we know it came into being.

On one level, Tlalteuctli's story joins with many creation stories from around the world in which an original god or goddess is slain and dismembered to create the world, serving to remind us of the necessity of continued sacrifice in the great chain, or web, of life. Plants rise from the remains of others, only to be eaten by animals who are then eaten by other animals. Youth is sacrificed to maturity, just as innocence is lost to wisdom. Nothing is gained without a loss in the economy of nature or psyche. From this perspective, illness, aging, and death are not breakdowns or failures of life; much the opposite, they ensure the continuance of life by feeding future generations and further stages of maturity. In my dream I held the index finger of my twin. She seemed to sustain me, even after her death. There was a sense that her murder would begin to awaken me from my youthful ignorance, my preference to remain innocent, unknowing, and blame-free.

That awakening has begun since the dream, stripping away the naive optimism and self-righteousness of my youth that could not encompass the presence of evil in this world, and in the best of us, including myself. This is the dark knowledge that is reflected by the black obsidian mirror of Nahuatl traditions. It is painful to see, and even more difficult to bear. I suspect that it is no coincidence—especially since I have heard similar tales from other sick people—that I came down with CFIDS after I remembered being molested as a child, worked with that memory in therapy, and finally comprehended its truth.

That truth holds impossible contradictions: that my abuser loved me and hurt me, that I sought his attentions while fearing his approach, that those who perpetuate abuse, and those who look away, are often good people who would not do those things intentionally, that violence occurs between parts of ourselves we do not claim and hardly remember. . . . Frankly, I do not know how to encompass these contradictory truths, or how those who have survived worse horrors than I manage to contain the much greater extremes of their experiences with any compassion, but I suspect that one of the tasks of illness is to find a way to do just that, to pick up the scattered pieces of the one who has been murdered, hold them in our arms, make the proper prayers, and lay them to rest.

This is not a task we can consciously perform; it is the soul's work, which may be why "the Earth opens up and swallows us" in the midst of crises like illness, "plunging us into the underworld where the soul resides, allowing us to dwell in darkness," as Gloria Anzaldúa has explained. "By keeping the conscious mind occupied or immobile, the germination work takes place in the deep, dark earth of the unconscious."[8] I suspect that much of this work occurs in our nighttime dreams, whether or not we remember them.

In the third year of my illness, I dreamed that I went to volunteer at a local hospital and the people there sent me to work in the "dead babies department," to talk to the grief-stricken parents and make prayers for all the babies who have died. When I woke up, I made that prayer, for the part of me that left or died when I was molested as a baby, and for all babies dying, or only partially surviving, of starvation, disease, abuse, neglect, or war. Sometimes I still make that prayer. I am intrigued by the fact that my dream instructed me to pray, and to pray not only for *my* lost child, but for *all* lost children; in so doing, I feel the sacredness of my being and of all other beings simultaneously, and come to see the universality of my experience. It feels as though the thin strand of my life is woven back into the web of our world. That may be the answer to my question of how to encompass the painful contradictions and injustices of life.

Stephen Levine has written of a woman named Hazel who had a similar realization during her terminal illness. Late one night, crazed with pain and bitterness of a lifetime of failed dreams, Hazel came to a point where she could no longer stand it. In the extremity of her anguish, she "began to experience all the other beings who at that very moment were lying in that same bed of agony": a starving mother in Ethiopia, an Eskimo woman dying in childbirth, a runaway teenager dying of hepatitis in a junky flat, a man crushed by a rockfall, lying on the banks of a river alone, and many more. "Something broke," she wrote of the experience. "Maybe it was my heart. But I saw it wasn't just *my* pain, it was *the* pain. It wasn't just my life, it was all life. It was life itself."[9] After that she was able to make peace with her family and her life, and die.

Tlalteuctli, on the other hand, has not found her peace and apparently still needs our prayers, for there is more to her story; it did not end with the beginning of the world. After she was torn apart and turned into all the fruits and features of the land, Tlalteuctli began to cry. She cried all night, every night—in fact, she still weeps at night—longing to eat human hearts. She would not be quiet until they were brought to her. To this day she will not be comforted or bear fruit until she has been drenched with human blood, that is, until proper offerings and sacrifices are made.

It seems, from this piece of Tlalteuctli's story, that some ruthless necessity or divine retribution was invoked by the violence of the original deed, the breach of a natural order, that began the world of human civilization as we know it. There is the sense that this chain of effects, Tlalteuctli's unending craving for hearts, continues long into the future, for as long as the story is needed and told. It is embedded in the soul of our world, what the ancient philosophers called the *anima mundi,* and each of us is allotted a small portion of that larger soul to work upon in our lives, in the ongoing process of creation. We each embody a piece of Tlalteuctli's suffering and hunger—that which is beyond comfort, locked in bitterness and fury—and assume the seemingly impossible task of mollifying it for the sake of us all. Perhaps it was with this understanding that medieval alchemists often insisted that "the one primarily in need of redemption is not man, but the deity who is lost and sleeping in matter."

Myths like this, in which an original goddess is destroyed by the gods of a conquering people, in this case the Aztecs, can also be read as descriptions of the rise of our present patriarchal civilizations, and as justifications for the continued oppression and sacrifice of innocents in our times. Tlalteuctli's craving for human hearts is an apt description of the ongoing, escalating cycle of destruction that characterizes our contemporary world. It eats our hearts out, destroying our capacity to feel anything for ourselves, each other, or the Earth that sustains us. Leslie Marmon Silko called it a "witchery" which was loosed upon the face of this continent a few hundred years ago and is still enacted by "destroyers" all around us and within us. She described these "destroyers" with imagery that echoes Tlalteuctli's story, noting "their highest ambition is to gut human beings while they are still breathing, to hold the heart still beating so the victim will never feel anything again. . . . Only destruction is capable of arousing a sensation, the remains of something alive in them; and each time they do it the scar thickens, and they feel less and less, yet still hungering for more."[10] Just as Tlalteuctli cries for human blood, so we have become bloodthirsty killers of our own kind and insatiable consumers of our world.

I hear Tlalteuctli calling to all of us belonging to the "civilized" world, reminding us of the violence that has been done—and of the sacrifices that must be made. Her story echoes through the centuries as the raging river of a curse that is also the cure, the unfulfilled promise, the unripened karma. Her dismembered parts represent all that we as individuals and as communities have cut off and buried or used for other purposes, in order to become who we are today. That includes everything from the trees that were felled for this paper, to the dreams we set aside to make our ways in the world; it also includes the ways we deny connections, make things separate, and isolate ourselves, feeling futile and irrelevant. For the witchery that binds our hearts and minds in twentieth-century America is the distorted belief that other creatures—be they insects or animals, blacks, whites, or Arabs—are enemies to make war upon, rather than members of the one being we all share. As I hold the finger of my dismembered twin, I begin to grasp all that I have lost, all that we have lost, and must regain.

SACRIFICE AND THE DEIFIED HEART

Tlalteuctli, weeping still, asks for a sacrifice. The shaman I consulted about my illness told me that I was a sacrifice, "dying so that others may live," and there are many sick people who feel themselves to be sacrificial lambs on the altar of medical progress, war, or technological development. Serious illnesses also force us to make sacrifices, to give up things we hold precious—not just the old TV in the closet, but our savings, marriage, mobility or pride, even our own flesh and blood. In making sacrifices, even unwillingly, we are reminded that nothing lasts forever or truly belongs to us; everything comes from and returns to an original source, in this case the body of Tlaltleuctli. The losses, provided we survive, make us more fully human, that is humble and caretaking, albeit limping, lonely, or poor. As the divine Mother of all gave her body so that we might live, so we must give of ourselves so that she may live in peace; this is the basic premise of religious sacrifice.

Joseph Epes Brown articulated this understanding of sacrifice in his discussion of the annual Sun Dance ceremonies performed by many Plains Indians, in which dancers pierce themselves "to honor all life and the source of all life." They do so, he explained, so that "all the world and humankind may continue on the path of the cycle of giving, receiving, bearing, being born in suffering, growing, becoming, returning to earth that which has been given, and finally being born again. Only in sacrifice is sacredness accomplished; only in sacrifice is identity found."[11]

I wonder whether the human predilection for murder, which is apparently unique to our species, is a desperate attempt to escape this fate, to sacrifice the body of another in place of one's own; in so doing, we maintain our "level of comfort" and illusions of power, but at the expense of our humanness. We become inhuman. Nature, which always works to redress imbalance, does not tolerate such hubris for long, as many Native American teachings and prophecies insist. "Such traditions," wrote Joseph Epes Brown, "affirm for those who listen, or indeed inevitably for those who do not, that where the sacred in the world and life is held as irrelevant illusion, where evasion of sacrifice in pursuit of some seeming 'good life' becomes a goal into itself, then . . . the ordering cycle of sacrifice will and must be accomplished by nature herself so that again there may be renewal in the world."[12] As I understand it, the "ordering cycle" of nature most often manifests as natural disasters and disease epidemics, for "she" sleeps and stirs in the bowels of the earth and our bodies. We have but one choice: to sacrifice or be sacrificed.

Now, sacrifice is a touchy subject for many people, myself included, who are trying to overcome Christian guilt or WASP conditioning, and especially for women with immune disorders, many of whom have a history of sacrificing themselves for others. Frankly, I could not take the idea seriously until I researched, and further understood, the Nahuatl concept of the "deified heart" that is worthy of sacrifice, and capable of nourishing and comforting Tlalteuctli.

The Nahuatl peoples believed that we are born with a physical heart, but have to create a deified heart by finding a firm and enduring center within ourselves from which to lead our lives, so that our hearts will shine through our faces, and our features will become reliable reflections of ourselves. Otherwise, they explained, we wander aimlessly through life, giving our hearts to everything and nothing, and so destroy them; I have yet to read a better definition of addiction or consumerism. Therefore, to sacrifice our hearts, in Nahuatl terms, is to consecrate ourselves; it is not to give ourselves away, but to keep ourselves true, by freeing our hearts from distraction and realigning ourselves with our appointed destinies. Ironically, we often find our true selves, and engage our souls, when our hearts are broken, bleeding, or sacrificed. As archeologist Laurette Séjourné explained in her study of Nahuatl religion, "to reach one's heart, to possess oneself of it, means to penetrate into spiritual life. The operation is extremely painful, and that is why the heart is always represented as wounded, and why the drops of blood issuing from it are so significant."[13]

With an eerie synchronicity, Jungian analyst Russell Lockhart reported that a client of his, who had just been diagnosed with leukemia, dreamed of a bleeding rose; the dreamer cupped his trembling hands and drank the blood dripping from the rose.[14] It is one of the strange paradoxes of illness, and mysteries of Tlalteuctli, that bleeding nourishes, and that suffering, when sanctified, can heal by resuscitating our hearts.

In our hearts, which many native peoples consider to be the seat of true intelligence, we discover the simple capacity to feel our losses, sorrow, and shame, and have compassion. We develop a "new tenderness for life," as Laura Chester noted, which many sick people count as the greatest blessing of their illnesses. "This gentleness," wrote Nancy Mairs, "is part of the reason that I'm not sorry to be a cripple. I didn't have it before."[15] It is the fruit of karma, the unwinding of results from more original causes, that finally comforts Tlalteuctli, lifts her curse upon the land and the people, and reinstates our connectedness with all things. I suspect that our bodies hold the memory of that collective curse in the very twisting matter of our genes, impelling resolution through cycling phases of health and illness, death and rebirth. For the physical imperatives of illness require the response of our hearts, the simple willingness to tend to ourselves and each other with patience, care, and the sense of preciousness that is born of loss.

The Navajo tell a beautiful story about the heart's role in healing in the Night Chant, which is recited in some curing rituals; Washington Matthews, the white anthropologist who first recorded it, named it the "Myth of the Stricken Twins."[16] In this story, two twin brothers, Monster Slayer and Born of Water, were blinded and lamed, respectively, by a rockfall while searching for the father they had never known, Talking God. Having become a burden upon their family, the twins were turned away and forced to wander, asking the gods, the Holy People, for help. Neither was able to travel alone, so they went together, providing eyes and legs for each other, in search of a cure. In the course of their journey, they met with fourteen refusals of help(!). Finally, the gods agreed to hold a curing ceremony; however, while the ceremony was in progress, the twins cried out in joy at the hope of being cured, breaking a stringent taboo against talking in the sweat lodge, so the ceremony immediately ceased, the gods departed, and the twins were left alone, still blind and lame.

In utter desperation, they began to cry, and from their cries they made a song:

From the white plain where stands the water,
From there we come.
Bereft of eyes, one bears another.
From there we come.
Bereft of limbs, one bears another.
From there we come.
Where healing herbs grow by the waters,
From there we come.
With these your eyes you shall recover.
From there we come.
With these your limbs you shall recover.
From there we come.

They sang with such heartfelt longing that the Holy People could not refuse, and they were finally restored to full health. (In some versions, the Holy People did not cure their physical ailments, but gave them magical powers instead.) And so we learn that the gods are mollified not by individual acts of heroism or endurance or even clever trickery, but by our simple willingness to join with another in bonds of mutual need and cry out from the depth of our longing, the sincerity of our hearts.

Of course, we are not always equal to the task, capable of longing, crying or singing, giving or receiving assistance; sometimes our hearts are shut tight with pain or bitterness. The continued trials and losses of chronic illness, like all adversities, strip away our margins for error and eliminate the easygoing trust, tolerance, and generosity of well-being. We get fussy, rigid, and particular about our ways and needs, beg for help while resisting intervention, complain bitterly, and take offense readily, in our wounded vulnerability. The places we cling to, hoarding rather than sharing, are often the places that must give way in the sacrifice: our pocketbooks, privacy, or pride. Doctor's visits usually take all three.

The nakedness of illness uncovers the particular ways our hearts have hardened into knots of judgment, impatience, and intolerance, as evidenced by the small cruelties that so often characterize our relations with ourselves and each other. The maddening interdependencies of the sick and the well (and the young and old, the rich and poor) force us to touch and accept our despised polarities, to search for our missing hearts, or pay the price in blood. For illness develops, as Navajo medicine woman Annie Kahn explains, from "the habit of excluding," which puts us off balance and out of harmony. "To heal, one must . . . accept. This very act causes healing."[17]

In the deepest and darkest part of my illness I had a dream that helped me to find that acceptance I so needed and turn it into (my version of) a song. In the dream a guide took me to see a film about the life of a woman who was sold into prostitution as a young girl and was nearly devastated by it; she grew up feeling ugly and degraded, having to sell herself to make her way, over and over again. The movie was very painful to watch, and when my guide asked me to watch it a second time, I refused. But she insisted, and so I watched it again. The second time around everything happened exactly as before, but I saw it differently; this time, I saw it all—the pain, ugliness, and injustice—as a story of the getting of wisdom.

Then the young woman herself appeared onstage. She gathered small objects, the kind of things that are found alongside roads—broken bottles, small stones, gum wrappers, flower petals, snail shells, and cigarette butts—to represent all the major experiences of her life, and placed them upon an altar as an offering. I was quite moved to realize that even the ugly, degraded affairs of our lives can be made into offerings, turned into something so holy as to be fit to feed the gods. In fact, I sensed that they belonged to the sacred all along; I simply had not known it.

I woke up a different person from that dream, feeling a sense of resolve around the facts of my life, and a compassion for all the parts and players, that has never gone away. That compassion is not one that forgets or even forgives; it simply acknowledges all things for what they are, in their totality. In the compass of that wisdom, rage winds down into mercy and reemerges as the searing blue flame of conscience. The experience reminded me of something that Laurette Séjourné wrote in explaining Nahuatl philosophy: ". . . the supreme task of human existence is to wrest the heart from its condition of self-destructive multiplicity. Because of this belief the Aztecs were accustomed to place a precious stone in the mouths of the dead, to represent the heart emerging, brilliant and pure, from the fire consuming the body."[18]

That which has been excluded and profaned must be redeemed as sacred; sacrifice, which translates as "making sacred," is the means to that end. To demean or deny any part of ourselves is to lose our hearts and souls; it is also to insult, anger, and starve the goddess who lives within our bodies and the earth itself. Healing inevitably springs from the parts of ourselves, and members of our communities, that have been shrouded with shame, and stolen from their rightful places in the realm of the sacred, the mouth of the goddess. Dreams and myths repeatedly insist that the lowliest among us provide the redemption we all need. In another Nahuatl creation story, it is the scabby one, Nanantzin, whose body is covered with oozing sores, who jumps in the fire to become the sun. In biblical terms, it is the stone that was rejected that becomes the cornerstone of new life. To heal ourselves and renew the world, we must retrieve that rejected stone, touch the untouchable within and without ourselves, and hold it as precious—which is not always easy.

SERVICING THE GODS

My dreams have repeatedly suggested that prayers and ritual offerings can help me to heal and retrieve the lost parts of myself, and I know I am not alone in that, for Russell Lockhart has observed that the dreams of sick people often involve what he terms a "call to ritual." These rituals, whether they are done in dreaming or waking life, are often very simple. Lockhart's client who dreamed of a bleeding rose simply reached out, cupping his trembling hands, to drink the blood. The young woman in my dream just placed the objects representing her life experiences upon an altar. Laura Chester wrote of meeting a woman with leukemia who woke up every night, went out into her garden, and simply gazed out into the sky. That was her ritual. After several nights, Chester reported, she realized that she kept returning her gaze to one particular star and felt herself falling in love with that star, looking forward to the time she would have with it in the middle of the night. "It was then that she began to perceive divine connection, the interweaving of all things, and she knew with her entire being that everything mattered—'Each feather that drops is felt in the universe, every death is acknowledged and received, and every life has its meaning.' " And, it turned out, her leukemia went into remission.

That story prompted Laura Chester to search for her way to pray, noting that "each person has to find her own style, her own expression—how to pray, how to ask, that was the hard part, humbling one's pride in order to ask." This was the task that the Stricken

Twins, whose story is retold in many Navajo curing ceremonies, also faced in their search for healing. Here is Chester's description of her process: "I found myself wanting to open my hands in the gesture of receiving, my head lifted rather than bowed. I still felt humble and small, yet glad in this upwardness, imagining light pouring into me, healing me, gathering me up and holding me, like an infant, given over. I could feel the need to bare the smallest part of myself, the tiny seed self, to expose what was essentially me, pitiful, painful, vulnerable, to hold that out, as if into shining rain."[19]

In so opening, acknowledging, and offering ourselves, with all our pain and longing, we feed the goddesses of the deep, who need us as much as we need them, and begin to heal. That is when Tlalteuctli is finally fed and comforted, and so willing to restore life to the land which is also her body. In fact, the Greek word for healing originally meant to "service the gods" and goddesses.[20] It is my belief that seriously ill and wounded individuals are beholden to the insulted gods and goddesses of the deep—who remember everything we as a people have forgotten or denied in the erasure of silence—and are required to minister to their miseries to bring relief for all. They search out the healing we all need, for sacrifices are traditionally offered to ensure future growth and fertility for the entire community of life.

Takánakapsâluk (also known as Sedna, Nuliajuk, and a vast array of other names in native tongues) is another insulted and dismembered goddess of the deep who is honored by the Inuit Indians of the Arctic. The stories and rituals associated with her have given me a strong and abiding image of the delicate ministering that is required of us in illness. I would like to finish by offering that image in the context of Takánakapsâluk's story, as described by Arctic explorer Knud Rasmussen in the early years of this century.[21]

Takánakapsâluk was known as "the Mother of the Sea Beasts." When she was a young woman, she was tricked into marrying a fulmar (a seagull-like bird); dutifully, she grabbed her sewing bag and went off to live with her husband in a faraway land. However, she was miserable there, missing her family and unaccustomed to the strange food and the constant cries of birds. So, when her father came to visit, Takánakapsâluk begged him to take her home, and he consented. They started back together in his boat, but her husband, the fulmar, pursued them and caused such a terrible storm to rise on the sea that Takánakapsâluk's father grew afraid and threw her overboard into the icy waters of the Arctic sea. Takánakapsâluk clung to the edge of the boat with the tips of her fingers; her father took his ax and chopped them off at the first knuckle. They fell into the sea and bobbed up as seals. Two more times Takánakapsâluk clutched the edge of the boat and each time her father hacked off her fingers at the next joint, which then became walruses and whales.

Finally, her father poked out one of her eyes, and Takánakapsâluk sank to the bottom of the sea, where she lives to this day in a small stone house, brooding over the destinies of men and women. A large and fierce dog with no tail guards the narrow entrance to her home. Inside, Takánakapsâluk sits with her back to a small fire, covered with an enormous tangle of black hair, crawling with lice; for without fingers, she cannot pick out lice, plait her hair, or sew. It is said that the thanklessness and broken promises of people collect like grease and dirt in her hair, making her miserable. Just outside her house, the beasts of the sea that sprang from the chopped-off pieces of her fingers—which the Inuit Indians rely upon for food, clothing, and fuel—can be heard puffing and rolling in a dragnet that only Takánakapsâluk can open.

The Inuit understood that whenever there is hunger and sickness among the people, it is because Takánakapsâluk is unhappy and so unwilling to release her creatures to the open sea where the hunters can find them. When that happened, the people asked their shaman to make the dangerous journey by trance to Takánakapsâluk's home at the bottom of the sea to ask her to send forth the seals, walruses, and whales. Inevitably, the shaman found Takánakapsâluk in a bad mood, complaining of the many transgressions of the people ashore, and set about mollifying her anger by carefully combing her hair and picking out the lice. If all went well, Takánakapsâluk would agree to release the sea creatures if the people above who have broken taboos confessed.

The shaman then returned from the deep, came out of his trance, and said to the members of the community gathered around him: "Let us hear." Slowly, one by one, everyone in the house confessed the infringements of taboo, the crimes against nature, of which they were guilty, crying out, "Perhaps it's my fault," until all the secrets were told, Takánakapsâluk was finally appeased, and the seals, walruses, and whales returned to the sea.

I think that "sure voice" I encounter when I get sick must belong to Takánakapsâluk or someone like her: the angry, insulted goddess of the sea the shaman told me lives in my womb. Takánakapsâluk holds the sea creatures in her net, just as Tlalteuctli holds the seeds in her fist, inhabiting the deep interiors of land and sea, body and psyche. They are heavy with the memories and bitterness of a forgotten past and periodically call us to our knees to make offerings, sacrifices, and amends, to mend our ways and unburden their miseries. Tlalteuctli demands our hearts; Takánakapsâluk asks for our careful attention and confessions.

Sometimes, especially when I am feeling tired and weary, burdened by the tasks of living, I think of the shaman who visited Takánakapsâluk, sitting by her side combing her hair, undoing the tangles, and picking out the lice that had multiplied in his absence. I imagine the task seemed overwhelming at first and took forever to accomplish; the very doing must have called forth a patience and tenderness in the shaman, even if he did not have it to begin with. That is the image of ministering that stays with me, for it describes what my illness requires of me.

The long hours in bed suspended between worlds take me over and over the tangled lines of my life, so many small things that got lost in the shuffle, speed, and striving of my adulthood: the messages that went ignored, the apologies I never made, the promises that were broken, the gratitude that was never spoken, the love—and resentments—I held to myself, the gardens that went untended, the gifts I received and set aside, the dreams I denied, unable to dare to believe in them. What a snarl! It is too late to go back to many of those friends and gardens, just as Takánakapsâluk cannot go back to get her fingers. They are gone for good. But I can pay attention, as the shaman did, to remember, mourn, and honor, to clear myself of these entangling lines while holding the entire snarl as sacred.

It is a tedious, tenuous, and life-giving labor. Grand, heroic gestures have no part in the process; in fact, they often make things worse by disrupting a delicate equilibrium. We have to be patient, take small steps, use few words, and treat ourselves with the tenderness of baby-catching hands, remembering that we find our power, our capacity to heal ourselves and our world, in our deep and abiding vulnerability.

When that snarl gets the better of me, when I'm so upset, wound up and knotted with rage, sorrow, or regret that I cannot rest, I walk down into the pasture in front of our house, find a place where the cows have trampled a path, making a soft bed of dirt, and lie down, face flat, on the earth. I go down slowly, first to my knees, as if in prayer, then on all fours, like an animal, and finally stretch myself out like a snake, until my stomach rests on the belly of the earth.

Lying there, with my face and fingers in the dirt, I empty myself out into the earth with whispers and tears until I finally come to rest and my breathing returns to normal. Then, and only then, do I become aware of my surroundings. I hear the calls, and see the shadows, of crows circling overhead, wondering if I am ready to eat. I feel the wind on my back, smell the scents of smoke and sage it carries, hear the stream running with snowmelt from the mountains, and watch the labor of ants hauling food back to their queens. Eventually I remember what I had once known and since forgotten:

that all of these beings—the running water, straining ants, and circling crows—are feeding, caressing, and cleaning the body of the earth, like the shaman who combs Takánakapsâluk's hair, simply by being who they are and doing what they do. When I finally stand up, and brush the dirt off my clothes, I know that nothing more is asked of me.

I hope I do not forget when I get well.

NOTES

INTRODUCTION

1. CFIDS, also known as CFS (chronic fatigue syndrome), CEBV (chronic Epstein-Barr virus), ME (myalgic encephalomyelitis), or the "yuppie flu," is a complex illness characterized by profound and prolonged fatigue, neurological problems, and a constellation of symptoms that resemble many immune disorders. These symptoms, as defined by the Centers for Disease Control, include low-grade fevers, sore throats, painful and swollen lymph glands, muscle weakness, joint and muscle pain, sleep disturbances, headaches, vision problems, forgetfulness, irritability, confusion, difficulty thinking, inability to concentrate, and depression. Patients also commonly report night sweats, shortness of breath, dizziness and balance problems, sensitivity to heat and cold, diarrhea, hair loss, allergies, and panic attacks. These symptoms tend to wax and wane but are often severely debilitating and may last for years. While all segments of the population are at risk, women under the age of forty-five seem to be the most susceptible; epidemiologists have estimated that, as of 1990, two to five million Americans had contracted CFIDS. For more information about the disease, contact the CFIDS Association, Inc., P.O. Box 220398, Charlotte, North Carolina 28222-0398, 1-800/442-3437.

2. Oliver Sacks, *A Leg to Stand On* (New York: Summit Books, 1984), p. 111.

3. Virginia Woolf, "On Being Ill," in *The Moment and Other Essays* (New York: Harcourt Brace Jovanovich, 1948), p. 11.

4. Margiad Evans, *A Ray of Darkness* (Dallas: Riverrun Press, 1952), p. 11.

1 THE INVISIBLE UNDERWORLD OF ILLNESS

1. Katherine Anne Porter, *Pale Horse, Pale Rider* (New York: New American Library, 1936), p. 158.

2. John Donne, "Devotions," in *Complete Poetry and Selected Prose of John Donne and Complete Poetry of William Blake* (New York: Random House, 1941), p. 309.

3. May Sarton, *After the Stroke: The Journal* (New York: W. W. Norton, 1988), p. 16.

4. Virginia Woolf, "On Being Ill," in *The Moment and Other Essays* (New York: Harcourt Brace Jovanovich, 1948), p. 9.

5. E. M. Cioran, "On Sickness," in *The Fall into Time* (New York: Quadrangle Books, 1970), p. 125.

6. Margiad Evans, *A Ray of Darkness* (Dallas: Riverrun Press, 1952), pp. 30, 131.

7. Simone de Beauvoir, *A Very Easy Death* (New York: G. P. Putnam's Sons, 1966), p. 79.

8. Carl Jung, *Memories, Dreams, Reflections* (New York: Pantheon, 1963), p. 292.

9. Evans, *A Ray of Darkness*, p. 131.

10. Nan Shin (Nancy Amphoux), *The Diary of a Zen Nun* (New York: E. P. Dutton, 1986), p. 80.

11. Woolf, "On Being Ill," p. 12.

12. Emily Dickinson, *Selected Poems and Letters of Emily Dickinson* (Garden City, NY: Doubleday & Company, 1959), p. 89.

13. Denton Welch, *A Voice Through a Cloud* (New York: E. P. Dutton, 1966), p. 18.

14. Elaine Scarry, *The Body in Pain: The Making and Unmaking of the World* (New York: Oxford University Press, 1985), pp. 33–34.

2 THE SECRETS OUR BODIES KEEP SAFE

1. Susan Griffin, "The Way of All Ideology," in *Made from This Earth* (New York: Harper & Row, 1982), pp. 164–65.

2. E. M. Cioran, "On Sickness," in *The Fall into Time* (New York: Quadrangle Books, 1970), p. 125.

3. Christiane Northrup, "Honoring Our Bodies," *Woman of Power*, no. 18, Fall 1990, p. 18.

4. Deepak Chopra, *Quantum Healing* (New York: Bantam Books, 1989), p. 142.

5. Elie Wiesel, *Twilight* (New York: Warner Books, 1987), p. 213.

6. Lewis E. Mehl, "Modern Shamanism: Integration of Biomedicine with Traditional World Views," in Gary Doore, ed., *Shaman's Path: Healing, Personal Growth and Empowerment* (Boston: Shambhala, 1988), p. 137.

7. Max Lerner, *Wrestling with the Angel* (New York: Simon & Schuster, 1990), p. 45.

8. Oliver Sacks, "Neurology and the Soul," *The New York Review of Books*, November 22, 1990, p. 49.

9. Susan Sontag, *Illness as Metaphor* (New York: Farrar, Straus, & Giroux, 1978), p. 54.

10. Marc Iverson, "In Response to Mr. Edelson," *The CFIDS Chronicle: Journal of the Chronic Fatigue and Immune Dysfunction Syndrome Association*, Spring 1989, p. 49.

11. Susan Griffin, quoted by Chellis Glendinning in *When Technology Wounds* (New York: William Morrow & Co., 1990), p. 156.

12. Morris Berman, *The Re-enchantment of the World* (New York: Bantam Books, 1984), p. 76.

3 TOXIC HEALTH: CULTURAL ASSUMPTIONS AND ILLUSIONS

1. Arnold Mindell, *Dreambody* (Santa Monica, CA: Sigo Press, 1982), pp. 113, 200.

2. For more information on cross-cultural perspectives on health and illness, see Gary Doore, ed., *Shaman's Path: Healing, Personal Growth and Empowerment* (Boston: Shambhala, 1988); Richard Grossinger, *Planet Medicine* (Berkeley, Calif.: North Atlantic Books, 1980); David S. Sobel, ed., *Ways of Health* (New York: Harcourt Brace Jovanovich, 1979); and Rachel E. Spector, *Cultural Diversity in Health and Illness* (New York: Appleton-Century-Crofts, 1979).

3. Quoted by Arthur Kleinman in *The Illness Narratives* (New York: Basic Books, 1988), p. 31.

4. Treya Killam Wilber, "When Bad Things Happen to Good People," *New Age Journal*, September/October 1988, p. 54.

5. Daniel Harris, "Life and Death: Some Meditations," *The Antioch Review*, Fall 1990, p. 427.

6. Adolf Guggenbuhl-Craig, "The Archetype of the Invalid and the Limits of Healing," *Spring: An Annual of Archetypal Psychology and Jungian Thought*, 1979, p. 37.

7. Mary Winfrey Trautmann, *The Absence of the Dead Is Their Way of Appearing* (Pittsburgh: Cleis Press, 1984), p. 162.

8. Virginia Woolf, "On Being Ill," in *The Moment and Other Essays* (New York: Harcourt Brace Jovanovich, 1948), p. 14.

9. Oliver Sacks, "Neurology and the Soul," *The New York Review of Books*, November 22, 1990, p. 45.

10. Terry Tempest Williams, "The Clan of One-Breasted Women," *Ms*, vol. 1, no. 2, September/October, 1991, p. 31.

11. Albert Kreinheder, *Body and Soul: The Other Side of Illness* (Toronto: Inner City Books, 1991), pp. 39–40.

12. Lewis E. Mehl, "Modern Shamanism: Integration of Biomedicine with Traditional World Views," in Doore, ed., *Shaman's Path*, p. 137.

13. Nancy Mairs, "On Being a Cripple," in *Plaintext: Deciphering a Woman's Life* (New York: Harper & Row, 1986), p. 20.

14. Fritjof Capra, *The Turning Point* (New York: Bantam Books, 1982), p. 103.

15. For more information on the development of medical science, see Jeanne Achterberg, *Woman as Healer* (Boston: Shambhala, 1991); Morris Berman, *The Re-enchantment of the World* (New York: Bantam Books, 1984); Capra, *The Turning Point*; Michel Foucault, *The Birth of the Clinic* (New York: Bantam Books, 1976); Thomas Goldstein, *The Dawn of Modern Science* (Boston: Houghton Mifflin, 1980).

16. Achterberg, *Woman as Healer*, p. 103.

17. Quoted in Barbara Ehrenreich and Deirdre English, *Witches, Midwives and Healers: A History of Women Healers* (Old Westbury, NY: The Feminist Press, 1973), p. 9.

18. William Barrett, *Death of the Soul: From Descartes to the Computer* (Garden City, NY: Anchor Books/Doubleday, 1986).

19. Mindell, *Dreambody*, p. 113.

20. René Dubos, *Mirage of Health* (Garden City, NY: Doubleday & Co., 1959, pp. 36–60.

21. Ibid., p. 13.

22. Carl Jung, *Alchemical Studies*, vol. 13, *The Collected Works of C. J. Jung*, The Bollingen Series XX (Princeton: Princeton University Press, 1968), par. 54.

23. Audre Lorde, *A Burst of Light* (Ithaca, NY: Firebrand Books, 1988), pp. 133–34.

24. Laura Chester, *Lupus Novice* (Berrytown, NY: Station Hill Press, 1987), p. 153.

25. Arnold Beisser, "Flying Without Wings," *New Age Journal*, March/April 1989, p. 88.

4 DANCING WITH DEATH: VEGETATIVE PROCESSES AT WORK

1. Quoted by Arnold Mindell in *Coma: Key to Awakening* (Boston: Shambhala, 1989), p. 44.

2. John Donne, "Devotions," in *Complete Poetry and Selected Prose of John Donne and Complete Poetry of William Blake* (New York: Random House, 1941), p. 311.

3. Max Lerner, *Wrestling with the Angel* (New York: Simon & Schuster, 1990), p. 175.

4. Mary Winfrey Trautmann, *The Absence of the Dead Is Their Way of Appearing* (Pittsburgh: Cleis Press, 1984), p. 175.

5. Steiner's philosophy is explained in A. C. Harwood, *The Recovery of Man in Childhood* (Spring Valley, NY: Anthroposophic Press, 1958), p. 56.

6. John Hobbie, "The Four Heavenly Messengers," *Inquiring Mind,* Summer 1990, p. 11.

7. Yaël Bethiem, "The Unhealed Life," *The Sun,* no. 158, January 1989, p. 38.

8. Nan Shin (Nancy Amphoux), *The Diary of a Zen Nun* (New York: E. P. Dutton, 1986), p. 80.

9. Treya Killam Wilber, "Do We Make Ourselves Sick?" *New Age Journal,* September–October 1988, p. 87.

10. I first encountered this redefinition of responsibility in Stephen and Ondrea Levine, "The Healing We Took Birth For," *Yoga Journal,* July/August 1987, p. 40.

11. Laura Chester, *Lupus Novice* (Berrytown, NY: Station Hill Press, 1987), p. 52.

12. E. M. Cioran, "On Sickness," in *The Fall into Time* (New York: Quadrangle Books, 1970), pp. 127–28.

13. Denton Welch, *A Voice Through a Cloud* (New York: E. P. Dutton, 1966), p. 209.

14. Oliver Sacks, *A Leg to Stand On* (New York: Summit Books, 1984), p. 170.

15. Traditional Iroquois dream theory is discussed by Anthony F. C. Wallace in "Dreams and the Wishes of the Soul: A Type of Psychoanalytic Theory Among Seventeenth Century Iroquois," in John Middleton, ed., *Magic, Witchcraft, and Curing* (Garden City, NY: The Natural History Press, 1967), pp. 171–90.

16. Audre Lorde, *A Burst of Light* (Ithaca, NY: Firebrand Books, 1988), p. 124.

17. Sandy Ingerman, "Contemporary Soul Retrieval: An Interview with Sandy Ingerman," *Shaman's Drum*, no. 24, Summer 1991, pp. 27–33.

18. Jeanne Achterberg, "The Wounded Healer: Transformational Journeys in Modern Medicine," in Gary Doore, ed., *Shaman's Path: Healing, Personal Growth and Empowerment* (Boston: Shambhala, 1988), p. 121.

19. Chester, *Lupus Novice*, p. 147.

5 THE ALCHEMY OF ILLNESS

1. Albert Kreinheder, *Body and Soul: The Other Side of Illness* (Toronto: Inner City Books, 1991), p. 88.

2. See Carl Jung, *Psychology and Alchemy*, vol. 12, *The Collected Works of C. G. Jung*, Bollingen Series XX, (New York: Pantheon, 1953; Princeton: Princeton University Press, 1968); Edward F. Edinger, *Anatomy of the Psyche* (La Salle, IL: Open Court Publishing Company, 1985); Liz Greene, "Alchemical Symbolism in the Horoscope," in Liz Greene and Harold Sasportas, *Dynamics of the Unconscious* (York Beach, Maine: Samuel Weiser, 1988); Charles Ponce, *Alchemy* (Berkeley, CA: North Atlantic Books, 1983); and Marie-Louise von Franz, *Alchemy* (Toronto: Inner City Books, 1980) and *Alchemical Active Imagination* (Dallas: Spring Publications, 1979).

3. Paracelsus, *Selected Writings*, ed. Jolande Jacobi, trans. Norbert Guterman (New York: Princeton University Press, 1951), pp. 143–44.

4. Ibid., p. 78.

5. Arnold Mindell, *Working with the Dreaming Body* (Boston: Routledge & Kegan Paul, 1985), p. 6.

6. Alice James, *The Diary of Alice James*, ed. and intr. Leon Edel (New York: Dodd, Mead and Company, 1964), p. 25.

7. Arnold Beisser, "Flying Without Wings," *New Age Journal*, March/April 1989, p. 50.

8. Laura Chester, *Lupus Novice* (Berryton, NY: Station Hill Press, 1987), p. 50.

9. Virginia Woolf, "On Being Ill," in *The Moment and Other Essays* (New York: Harcourt Brace Jovanovich, 1948), p. 12.

10. Mary Winfrey Trautmann, *The Absence of the Dead Is Their Way of Appearing* (Pittsburgh: Cleis Press, 1984), p. 19.

11. John Donne, "Devotions" in *Complete Poetry and Selected Prose of John Donne and Complete Poetry of William Blake* (New York: Random House, 1941), p. 335.

12. Robert Murphy, *The Body Silent* (New York: W. W. Norton, 1988), pp. 42–43.

13. Ibid., p. 66.

6 THE UNDERWORLD JOURNEY

1. Oliver Sacks, *A Leg to Stand On* (New York: Summit Books, 1984), p. 133.

2. For more information on the structure of initiations in myth and practice, see Joseph Campbell, *The Hero with a Thousand Faces* (Princeton: Princeton University Press, 1949); Arnold van Gennep, *The Rites of Passage* (London: Routledge and Kegan Paul, 1909); J. S. La Fontaine, *Initiation* (New York: Viking Penguin, 1985); Louise Carus Mahdi, Steven Foster and Meredith Little, eds., *Betwixt and Between* (La Salle, Ill.: Open Court Publishing Company, 1987); R. J. Stewart, *The Underworld Initiation* (Guildford, England: The Aquarian Press, 1985); and Victor Turner, *The Ritual Process* (Ithaca, N.Y.: Cornell University Press, 1969).

3. Toni Cade Bambara, *The Salt-Eaters* (New York: Random House, 1980), p. 247.

4. Audre Lorde, *A Burst of Light* (Ithaca, NY: Firebrand Books, 1988), p. 121.

5. Denton Welch, *A Voice Through a Cloud* (New York: E. P. Dutton, 1966), p. 54.

6. Yaya Diallo and Mitchell Hall, *The Healing Drum: African Wisdom Teachings* (Rochester, VT: Destiny Books, 1989), p. 64.

7. Carl Jung, *Memories, Dreams, Reflections* (New York: Pantheon, 1963), p. 292.

8. John G. Neihardt, *Black Elk Speaks* (New York: William Morrow & Company, 1932), p. 36.

9. Mary Winfrey Trautmann, *The Absence of the Dead Is Their Way of Appearing* (Pittsburgh: Cleis Press, 1984), pp. 160–61.

10. Gerhard Dorn, quoted in Marie-Louise von Franz, *Alchemical Active Imagination* (Dallas: Spring Publications, 1979), p. 55.

11. Jung, *Memories, Dreams, Reflections,* p. 297.

12. Lorde, *A Burst of Light,* p. 134.

7 SHAME AND THE WHITE SHADOW OF THE COLLECTIVE

1. Stephen Larsen, *The Shaman's Doorway* (New York: Harper & Row, 1976), p. 162.

2. John Donne, "Devotions" in *Complete Poetry and Selected Prose of John Donne and Complete Poetry of William Blake* (New York: Random House, 1941), p. 332.

3. Chief Seattle, "Chief Seattle Address," *Santa Fe Spirit Magazine,* December/January 1990–91, pp. 29–30.

4. Fritjof Capra, *The Turning Point* (New York: Bantam Books, 1982), p. 103.

5. Patricia Frances Sargent, *Dimensions of Shame: An Heuristic Study from the Perspective of Feminine Consciousness* (Ann Arbor, MI: University Microfilms International, 1982).

6. Primo Levi, *The Drowned and the Saved* (New York: Summit Books, 1988), pp. 72–73.

7. Quoted in Mark P. O. Morford and Robert J. Lenardon, *Classical Mythology,* 2d ed. (New York: Longman, 1977), p. 43.

8. Quoted in Chellis Glendinning, *When Technology Wounds* (New York: William Morrow & Company, 1990), p. 64.

9. Yaël Bethiem, "The Unhealed Life," *The Sun,* no. 158, January 1989, p. 38.

10. Audre Lorde, *A Burst of Light* (Ithaca, NY: Firebrand Books, 1988), p. 59.

11. Nancy Mairs, "On Being a Cripple," in *Plaintext: Deciphering a Woman's Life* (New York: Harper & Row, 1986), p. 20.

12. Ken Wilber, "Do We Make Ourselves Sick?" *New Age Journal*, September/October 1988, p. 86.

13. Arnold Mindell, *Dreambody* (Santa Monica, CA: Sigo Press, 1982), p. 59.

14. Red Iron, "An Interview with Governor Alexander Ramsey of Minnesota, 1852," Wayne Moquin, ed., with Charles Van Doren, *Great Documents in American History* (New York: Praeger Publishers, 1973), p. 164.

15. Leslie Marmon Silko, *Ceremony* (New York: Viking Penguin, 1977), p. 69.

16. Mary Winfrey Trautmann, *The Absence of the Dead Is Their Way of Appearing* (Pittsburgh: Cleis Press, 1984), pp. 49–50.

17. Alice Bailey, *Esoteric Healing* (New York: Lucis Publishing Company, 1951), p. 30.

18. Deepak Chopra, *Quantum Healing* (New York: Bantam Books, 1989), p. 267.

19. Russell A. Lockhart, "Cancer in Myth and Dream," in *Words as Eggs* (Dallas: Spring Publications, 1983), p. 71.

20. Marie-Louise von Franz, *On Dreams and Death* (Boston: Shambhala, 1987), p. 109.

8 MYTHOLOGY AND THE DARK HEART OF HEALING

1. Susan Griffin, *Unremembered Country* (Port Townsend, WA: Copper Canyon Press, 1987), pp. 122–23.

2. Oliver Sacks, *A Leg to Stand On* (New York: Summit Books, 1984), p. 113.

3. For more information about underworld goddesses, see: Gloria Anzaldúa, *Borderlands/La Frontera* (San Francisco: Sisters/Aunt Lute Book Company, 1987); Demetra George, *Mysteries of the Dark Moon* (San Francisco: Harper San Francisco, 1992); Judith Gleason, *Oya: In Praise of the Goddess* (Boston: Shambhala, 1987); Ajit Mookerjee, *Kali: The Feminine Force* (New York: Destiny Books, 1988); Sylvia Brinton Perera, *Descent to the Goddess* (Toronto: Inner City Books, 1981); and Barbara Walker, *The Crone* (San Francisco, Harper & Row, 1985).

4. Toni Cade Bambara, *The Salt-Eaters* (New York: Random House, 1980), p. 19.

5. Anzaldúa, *Borderlands/La Frontera,* p. 46.

6. Albert Kreinheder, *Body and Soul: The Other Side of Illness* (Toronto, Inner City Books, 1991), pp. 34–35.

7. My sources for information on Tlalteuctli are: Burr Cartwright Brundage, *The Fifth Sun* (Austin: University of Texas Press, 1979); Joseph Campbell, *Historical Atlas of World Mythology,* vol. 2, pt. 3: "Mythologies of the Primitive Planters: The Middle and Southern Americas" (New York: Harper & Row, 1989); Alfonso Caso, *The Aztecs: People of the Sun* (Norman: University of Oklahoma Press, 1958); and Ptolemy Tompkins, *This Tree Grows Out of Hell* (San Francisco: Harper San Francisco, 1990).

8. Anzaldúa, *Borderlands/La Frontera,* p. 47.

9. Stephen Levine, *Healing into Life and Death* (Garden City, N.Y.: Anchor Books/Doubleday, 1987), pp. 12–13.

10. Leslie Marmon Silko, *Ceremony* (New York: Viking Penguin, 1977), pp. 229, 230.

11. Joseph Epes Brown, *The Spiritual Legacy of the American Indian* (New York: Crossroad Publishing Company, 1982), p. 105.

12. Ibid., p. 101.

13. Laurette Séjourné, *Burning Water* (New York: Thames & Hudson, 1956), p. 121.

14. Russell Lockhart, "Metaphor as Illness," in *Words as Eggs* (Dallas: Spring Publications, 1983), p. 213.

15. Nancy Mairs, "On Being a Cripple," in *Plaintext: Deciphering a Woman's Life,* (New York: Harper & Row, 1986), p. 20.

16. My primary sources for the "Myth of the Stricken Twins" are Donald Sandner, *Navajo Symbols of Healing* (New York: Harcourt Brace Jovanovich, 1979), and Susan Scarberry-Garcia, *Landmarks of Healing* (Albuquerque: University of New Mexico Press, 1990).

17. Quoted in Bobette Perone, H. Henrietta Stockel, and Victoria Krueger,

Medicine Women, Curanderas, and Women Doctors (Norman: University of Oklahoma Press, 1989), p. 36.

18. Séjourné, *Burning Water,* p. 73.

19. Laura Chester, *Lupus Novice* (Berrytown, NY: Station Hill Press, 1987), pp. 77–78.

20. Lockhart, "Metaphor as Illness," p. 59.

21. My sources for Takánakapsâluk's stories are: Franz Boas, *The Central Eskimo* (Lincoln: University of Nebraska, 1964); Mircea Eliade, *Shamanism* (New York: Pantheon Books, 1964); Gael Hodgkins, "Sedna: Images of the Transcendent in an Eskimo Goddess" in Rita M. Gross, ed., *Beyond Androcentrism* (New York: Scholar's Press, 1981); and Stephen Larsen, *The Shaman's Doorway* (New York: Harper & Row, 1976).

ABOUT THE AUTHOR

Kat Duff is a fifth-generation Minnesotan. She received a B.A. from Hampshire College, Massachusetts, in literature and women's studies in 1974. In her twenties she worked as a special education teacher, a printer, and a baker. In 1982 she entered graduate school and two years later received a combined M.A. in counseling and education from Southwestern College in Santa Fe, New Mexico. She makes her home in northern New Mexico

OTHER BELL TOWER BOOKS

Valeria Alfeyeva. PILGRIMAGE TO DZHVARI: *A Woman's Journey of Spiritual Awakening.* Hardcover 0-517-59194-4 (1993).

David A. Cooper. SILENCE, SIMPLICITY, AND SOLITUDE: *A Guide for Spiritual Retreat.* Hardcover 0-517-58620-7 (1992).
——. THE HEART OF STILLNESS: *The Elements of Spiritual Practice.* Hardcover 0-517-58621-5 (1992).
——. ENTERING THE SACRED MOUNTAIN: *A Mystical Odyssey.* Hardcover 0-517-59653-9 (1994).

James G. Cowan. LETTERS FROM A WILD STATE: *Rediscovering Our True Relationship to Nature.* Hardcover 0-517-58770-X (1992).
——. MESSENGERS OF THE GODS: *Tribal Elders Reveal the Ancient Wisdom of the Earth.* Softcover 0-517-88078-4 (1993).

Marc David. NOURISHING WISDOM: *A Mind/Body Approach to Nutrition and Well-Being.* Hardcover 0-517-57636-8 (1991); Softcover 0-517-88129-2 (1994).

Noela N. Evans. MEDITATIONS FOR THE PASSAGES AND CELEBRATIONS OF LIFE: *A Book of Vigils.* Hardcover 0-517-59341-6 (1994).

Burghild Nina Holzer. A WALK BETWEEN HEAVEN AND EARTH: *A Personal Journal on Writing and the Creative Process.* Softcover 0-517-88096-2 (1994).

Greg Johanson and Ron Kurtz. GRACE UNFOLDING: *Psychotherapy in the Spirit of the Tao-te ching.* Hardcover 0-517-58449-2 (1991); Softcover 0-517-88130-6 (1994).

Marcia and Jack Kelly. SANCTUARIES—THE NORTHEAST: *A Guide to Lodgings in Monasteries, Abbeys, and Retreats of the United States.* Softcover 0-517-57727-5 (1991).
——. SANCTUARIES—THE WEST COAST AND SOUTHWEST. Softcover 0-517-88007-5 (1993).
——. ONE HUNDRED GRACES, eds., with calligraphy by Christopher Gausby. Hardcover 0-517-58567-7 (1991).

Barbara Lachman. THE JOURNAL OF HILDEGARD OF BINGEN. Hardcover 0-517-59169-3 (1993).

Gunilla Norris. BEING HOME: *A Book of Meditations.* Hardcover 0-517-58159-0 (1991).
——. BECOMING BREAD: *Meditations on Living and Transformation.* Hardcover 0-517-59168-5 (1993).
——. SHARING SILENCE: *Meditation Practice and Mindful Living.* Hardcover 0-517-59506-0 (1993).

Ram Dass and Mirabai Bush. COMPASSION IN ACTION: *Setting Out on the Path of Service.* Softcover 0-517-57635-X (1991).

Richard Whelan, ed. SELF-RELIANCE: *The Wisdom of Ralph Waldo Emerson as Inspiration for Daily Living.* Softcover 0-517-58512-X (1991).

Bell Tower books are for sale at your local bookstore,
or you may call 1-800-733-3000 to order with a credit card.